underground **books**

The View From Lawrence Ferlinghetti's Bathroom Window_

Ron Whitehead

printed in NYC 2019

ISBN: 978-1-7322097-1-8

Front cover photo of Lawrence Ferlinghetti & Ron Whitehead, Ferlinghetti's front door, San Francisco, California, May 1993 by Nancye Browning.

Back cover photo of Lorenzo and Lawrence Ferlinghetti, Ron Whitehead, Kent Fielding, & Ron Seitz, Twice Told Books, Bardstown Road, Louisville Kentucky, on our way to visit Thomas Merton's grave at the Abbey of Gethsemani, April 1993 by C. Coddington.

Front and Back Cover Art and Design by James Browning Kepple w/ help from Max Kurganskyy

Text/Art Design by James Browning Kepple

The View from Lawrence Ferlinghetti's Bathroom Window:

Poems, Stories, Interviews, and Photos: From The Beat to The Underground

by Ron Whitehead

The View from Lawrence Ferlinghetti's Bathroom Window

Poems, Stories, Interviews, and Photos
From The Beat to The Underground

by Ron Whitehead

Other UB titles by Ron Whitehead:

DISOBEY by Ron Whitehead & Jinn Bug

A Taoist Nun Teaches Me in Fourteen Poems by Ron Whitehead

The Path of The Ancient Skald by Ron Whitehead

Underground Books/UB

New York City / Houston / Kyiv

www.undergroundbooks.org

The View from Lawrence Ferlinghetti's Bathroom Window:
Poems, Stories, Interviews, and Photos
From The Beat to The Underground
Ron Whitehead - 1st ed. ISBN-978-1-7322097-1-8

Some of these works have appeared in other publications, too numerous to mention, around the world. Thank you to each and every publisher.

Front cover photo by Nancye Browning. Back cover photo by C. Coddington.

Special thanks to my beloved Jinn Bug for photos, and especially for walking with me every step of the way! www.jinnbug.com

Underground Books/UB

New York City

UB website: www.undergroundbooks.org

Ron Whitehead website: www.tappingmyownphone.com

Table of Contents:

THE VIEW FROM LAWRENCE FERLINGHETTI'S BATHROOM WINDOW: SAN FRANCISCO, MAY 1993

for Lawrence Ferlinghetti, on his 100th Birthday, 3/24/19

visited Lawrence Ferlinghetti
flew to San Francisco
super shuttled to City Lights
keys at the front desk
with address and map
wandered streets Kerouac Alley Kenneth Rexroth Place
lost for hours
small suitcase weighed down with
heavy words "The Mask is the Path of the Star"
Diane di Prima's chapbook
Published in Heaven Series White Fields Press
limited edition of 50 copies to meet her
and have them signed
where is Diane di Prima
on Laguna Haight-Asbury San Francisco Art Institute
"the only war that matters is the war against the imagination"
and I'm searching for Diane di Prima
where is Lawrence Ferlinghetti
from his bathroom window
I see Golden Gate Bridge and Alcatraz
where is Lawrence Ferlinghetti
on Francisco Telegraph Hill North Beach City Lights
"Poets come out of your closets
open your windows, open your doors,
You have been holed up too long
In your closed worlds..."
and I'm searching for Lawrence Ferlinghetti
walked Golden Gate Bridge
into the wind
Alcatraz and sailboats one bent

licking the lips of the Bay waters
and the Pacific sprays tears
of Chinese immigrants who for forty days
and forty nights have stood on water
outside America's door knocking
denied entry denied
Fisherman's Wharf seals singing
some burnt out old hippie screeching "I am a Rock
I am an Island" for spare change from laughing

lines of tourists from around the world waiting
for trolley tours lunch at Fish Alley
hike up Telegraph Hill
what a view but
a statue of Columbus? is this
is this a Columbus I don't know about?
the other Columbus? The San Francisco
Telegraph Hill North Beach Columbus?
Father Christopher Columbus of
Our Lady of the Flowers?
no, Lawrence Ferlinghetti says
this is THE Christopher Columbus.
"We tried to spray paint his
hands red but PoliceMen
surrounded him all night
Columbus Day Eve."
Christopher Columbus Chief Joseph
two histories
"Hear me, my chiefs. I am tired: my heart
is sick and sad. From where the sun now
stands, I will fight no more forever."
walking up hills bowing to gravity
leaning backward with my long hair sweeping pigeon shit
from the path
as I descend the wind and the descent flatten me
and now my muscles are green and yellow and red pain
Caffe Puccini Caffe Verdi Caffe Trieste
espresso cappuccino
Chinatown fresh fruit and vegetables
the smell of dead animals "whole schools of fish,"

bulging eyes, "gasping on counters" whispering
Unheard
T'ai chi in the parks on the streets
movement before sunrise speeding speeding into
America
Hong Kong mutant flu killer virus
now after noon what do they think of me
walking here what do I look like to them
so different so alike
I want love to have its way
is their society still as closed as Bruce Lee found it
in 1962 North Beach and Oakland and Sacramento
like kudzu Hong Kong money buying out the Italians
buying San Francisco

and searching for Lawrence Ferlinghetti
I crawl through City Lights
so many writers' writings
and Lawrence Ferlinghetti is one
and James Joyce is one
and William Carlos Williams is one
and William Butler Yeats is one
and Walt Whitman is one
and William Blake is one
and Jack Kerouac Allen Ginsberg
Neal Cassidy William S. Burroughs
Diane di Prima Amiri Baraka
John Holmes Herbert Huncke
Gregory Corso Michael McClure
Gary Snyder Robert Creeley
Phillip Lamantia David Amram
Anne Waldman Ed Sanders
Hunter S. Thompson Charles Bukowski
Ken Kesey Bob Dylan
Tom Waits Nick Cave
Shane McGowan Ron Whitehead
Pomes Penyeach
Pomes All Sizes
"street poetry"
casting off "the anxiety of influence"

"the anxiety of authorship"
"Make it New!"
"First thought, best thought"
"have an uninterrupted curiosity"
"writing the mind"
"poet get out of the
inner aesthetic sanctum
where you have too long
been contemplating
your complicated navel"
and as I search for Lawrence Ferlinghetti
feed the cat and look at photo of Allen Ginsberg and
Lorenzo swimming
Julie
why do men still drink wine
and women still water
Daniel Ortega's Minotaur keeps watchful eye over
apartment stairs and Liberty's mask
like a gargoyle

guards his bedroom
paintings and posters of readings round the world
cover the walls
Travels in America Deserta on the shelf
Alcatraz in the distance
3rd World Voices monks Ernesto Cardenal Nicanor Parra
Daniel Berrigan Thomas Merton pierce the world's terrors
chanting Shelley's "Declaration of Rights"
"Government has no rights; it
is a delegation from several
individuals for the purpose of
securing their own."
and searching for Lawrence Ferlinghetti
I look in A Coney Island of the Mind
and Pictures of the Gone World
bearing gifts I come
photos of his journey through Kentucky
standing at Merton's grave Literary Gethsemani
memories of drinking Budweisers
at The Do Drop Inn

"Nice People Dancing to Good Country Music"
and I've come bearing gifts
tapes of his reading in Louisville
jazz between poems
silence between poems
blank spaces on the walls between paintings
and My Old Kentucky Home
is still singing your song
and I'm searching for Lawrence Ferlinghetti
"the one who'll shake the ones unshaken
the fearless one
the one without bullshit"
and walking out his front door
from Bolinas from Lorenzo from trees and backroads
he arrives in an old white Toyota truck
ascetic monk of North Beach
satirical wit ironic humor
Wisdom
southern hospitality in San Francisco California
handing Lawrence Ferlinghetti his keys end of visit
shaking hands saying thanks homage
super shuttle to airport Kentucky
and searching for Lawrence Ferlinghetti
on the plane I read from the book he signed

"Christ climbed down
from His bare tree
this year
and softly stole away into
some anonymous Mary's womb again
where in the darkest night
of everybody's anonymous soul
He awaits again
an unimaginable
and impossibly
Immaculate Reconception
the very craziest
of Second Comings."

Happy 100th Birthday my friend Lawrence Ferlinghetti!
Congratulations on your new book:
Little Boy: A Novel!
I hope you receive The Nobel Prize
for Literature this Year!

CAN A POET BE AN OUTLAW?

Who the fuck cares?
Poets do, readers do.

Poets define, make metaphors, unravel
imponderables, indisputables, mysteries

Poets bend and twist, shape and dance
on the certainty of sensory sensation.

I am not talking about representation,
the singularity of origin,

an assimilated sense of meaning
which is different for everyone,

or a central 'idea' of anything.
If she is not an outlaw poet no one is an outlaw.

She fearlessly stands outside your laws
and tells it like it is.

Only a dick would start an argument
on semantics or denounce the poet's concepts

as she chooses to represent them.

This is her tradition.

She is a contrarian
in the best sense of the word.

I could care less
what a dictionary defines as outlaw.

I could care less
about the definition of any word

other than how the outlaw poet uses it,
feels it, burns it, tattoos it into her skin.

That is what we deal with.
The outlaw poet's words.

What a petty discussion.
The poet says she is outlaw,

and I know her
and I'm willing to give her

her word.
She's an outlaw with words.

Her words can kill
or make thousands sing along.

She has lived it. She lives it.
She is wise.

She knows when to pull her gun
and it's not arbitrary.

She speaks and lives the truth.
She shoots words of truth.

Might not be yours
but she tells it like a motherfucker.

She's not this generation's Elizabeth Barrett Browning.
So what if sometimes she's drunk,

wailing madwoman,
she is that kind of writer.

She's the new Kentucky prophet.
She'll fuck them in their still wet eyes

and fill their skulls with urine.
That's her outlaw poetry.

Collect her piss as souvenir,
and study it

in whatever university will buy it.
She's right here,

standing, reading, shouting
her revolutionary poetry, outlaw poems.

Let her be! Let her go!

She will still stand

and write and roll.
She is

our Lorde, our Rich, our Plath, our di Prima, our Angelou,
our Percy, our Atwood, our Waldman, our Walker,

She brings her friends with her.
She is a general,

a Jesus-Muhammad-Buddha general.
Love General.

She is America's outlaw poet.
She'll kill you with love.

She'd rather hug your ass
than put a bullet in it.

CALLING THE TOADS
The Antinomian Fire This Time

by John Tytell and Ron Whitehead

the bone man dances circles
round the subterranean gloom
paints pink and blue and purple
until he fills the room
with the smell of roses
and a pandemonium moon

There is a struggle going on for our minds the minds of The World People. Every form of expression is being attacked. The attack is overt and subtle, explicit and implicit. The attack manifests as silent persecution, as mind manipulation, as censorship, as fear. The attack is pervasive. Most people, being asleep, are not even aware of the attack - until their doors are broken down. In the face of fear the poet the writer the artist the composer the musician the filmmaker can and must speak must act. I believe in individuals who are awake who fight for freedom. I believe in non-violent fighting which creates new forms new voices which, by their own being and expression and action, stand against reaction against fundamentalism against violence against war.

UNSCREW THE LOCKS FROM THE DOORS
UNSCREW THE DOORS FROM THEIR JAMBS

Anne Hutchinson, William Blake, Walt Whitman &
The Antinomian Tradition

VOICES WITHOUT RESTRAINT

"Government shall make no law respecting an establishment of
religion, or prohibiting the free exercise thereof; or abridging the
freedom of speech, or of the press; or the right of the people peaceably to
assemble, and to petition the government for a redress of grievances."
 -The Bill of Rights, 1st Amendment

Anne Hutchinson, cousin of John Dryden, organized a circle of women and led
them in discussions of church sermons. The notion that women would even
dare to discuss these sermons was considered subversive - after all,
discussion leads to questions. Anne Hutchinson was convicted of "traducing"
the ministry and banished, cast out of Boston.

Antinomian emerges from the Protestant Reformation which encourages its
adherents to deny authority and resist the state when its moral position is
feeble, contradictory, absurd. In legal terminology an antinomy signifies a
contradiction which in Walt Whitman's historical moment was the condition of
slavery in a supposedly free society.

"The attitude of great poets is to cheer up slaves and horrify despots," Whitman
wrote. He, like William Blake before him, saw his purpose as spreading to the
people the original ideas of the American republic, and a revolution that had
been fought to relocate sovereignty in the individual rather than in the state. In
an editorial he declared that the greatest evil was "strife for gain," yet even in
his crusading journalism he was a voice of affirmation and love.

"Unscrew the locks from the doors,
Unscrew the doors from their jambs"
-Whitman

"Poetry fettered fetters the human race"
-Blake

"

It is not metres, but a metre-making argument that makes a poem"
-Emerson

"Urge and urge and urge. Always the procreant urge of the world"
-Whitman

"through the windr of a wondr in a wildr is a weltr as a wirble of a warbl is a world"
-Joyce

When Whitman completed LEAVES OF GRASS, the grass being the uncut hair of the dead, he designed it, set some of his own type, and set as his publication date the fourth of July, 1855.

LEAVES OF GRASS was disdained by critics as "a mass of stupid filth," an example of "New York Rowdyism," "grotesque and uncouth." The only favorable reviews were written by Whitman himself, pseudonymously, except that is for a letter from Emerson proclaiming Whitman's book as the "most extraordinary piece of wit and wisdom that America has yet contributed." After Whitman was debilitated by stroke the young Henry James attacked his work and a generation later, in a jealous attempt to dethrone the cosmic poet who had written the American epic poem of the 19th Century, Ezra Pound continued the attack on Whitman's romanticism.

Whitman revised and expanded his poems for the rest of his life but not before paying over six hundred visits to hospital wards during the American Civil War. Basic surgery was amputation. Suffering was overwhelming. Whitman maintained cheerful optimism, the hallmark of his character. Whitman gave succor to the wounded.

Pound's CANTOS reflect his own lifetime of antinomian resistance to the warfare state. Long after he made his peace with Whitman, Pound became pariah of modern poetry, hysterically protesting "a system which created one war after another in series in system." Ezra Pound was incarcerated, twelve years in the house of bedlam, St. Elizabeth's, an asylum for the criminally insane in Washington D.C., which, years earlier, during the Civil War, had been one of the hospitals for the wounded visited by Whitman.

Another antinomian, arriving in Paris, 1930, with ten dollars and a copy of LEAVES OF GRASS, forty years old, twenty unsuccessful years trying to write fiction during an anguished marriage, liberated himself from the middle class values most take for granted, destitute, surviving by persuading a dozen new friends to feed and house him in rotation in exchange for his conversation, fell in love with Anais Nin, another unknown writer, and began his first masterpiece, TROPIC OF CANCER.

In his poems Whitman simultaneously praised and condemned his country. In CANCER Henry Miller savages America as a "cesspool of the spirit," "a curse on the world." While Whitman introduced orgasmic potential in "Song of Myself" Miller used sexual liberation as antinomian metaphor. Published in Paris, 1934, CANCER didn't appear in an American edition until 1960 when Miller was past 70. Whitman's poems were challenged by the district attorney of Boston but Miller's CANCER faced 50 obscenity charges resolved finally by the Supreme Court. One of the triggers of the Sixties.

Ezra Pound, an iconoclast far on the right of the political spectrum. Henry Miller, a Nietzchean nihilist with an anarchistic distrust of all institutions. Both romantics who cannot believe with Whitman in the dream of American possibility.

Whitman, Pound, Miller, all Voices Without Restraint. Crucial American influences on The Beat Generation. The Beat Generation. In the next decade The Beat Generation will come to be recognized as the most important group of poets and writers in the history of America. Jack Kerouac, spokesperson for The Beat Generation wrote a panoramic rhapsody infused with Whitman's identification with the common, the lowly, the downtrodden. Kerouac eulogizes his hoboes and wanderers in the same natural speech which caused James Russell Lowell to keep Whitman off the shelves at Harvard. Kerouac's prose line, his long, endlessly unpunctuated, surging sentences are based on Whitman's "Song of Myself" and like Whitman Kerouac is a celebrant who remains optimistic, despite all odds, despite all suffering struggle pain failure, he remains optimistic because he knows the journey is perpetual and has no end.

Kerouac's friend Allen Ginsberg is even closer to Whitman. "Howl," written exactly a century after "Song of Myself," uses the same long line. In Whitman's case as in Ginsberg's form becomes a function of the freedom to which the poet aspires. The holy, holy, holy, everything is holy is magnificent Whitman AH and AHA ecstasy.

Ginsberg is less ambivalent than Whitman about the human price we pay for commerce and industry, more in accord with Pound and Miller in his suspicion of Moloch, his cannibal dynamo of industry named after the Babylonian god to whom children were sacrificed. But Ginsberg's antinomianism has been, like Whitman's, the wound dresser, adhesive, sewing a communal purpose. So Ginsberg helped organize the peace marchers in the Sixties, was witness to the Chicago National Convention in 1968, along with his friend William S. Burroughs, who may be the most antinomian of all The Beats.

Lawrence Ferlinghetti, who was arrested for publishing "Howl," Ferlinghetti, whose City Lights Books is antinomian mecca of the world, Ferlinghetti, whose A CONEY ISLAND OF THE MIND has sold more copies than any book of poetry by any living American poet, Ferlinghetti, antinomian to the end, sees the poet as enemy of the state.

The antinomian legacy of Whitman, Pound, Miller, Kerouac, Ginsberg, Burroughs, Ferlinghetti, and so many other poets, writers, artists, musicians, filmmakers leads to our door and in this final moment having stood in the shadows for too long we step out and now we stand on the

brink on the edge
at the ending of time

Time was Time is Time will be no more
and it's The Big Bang Epiphany
in the gap between thought and image
Voices streams racing
whispering through our blood
pleading through our bones
strange activities of our nerves
the unconscious life of our minds
a tetrameter of iambs marching
shouting Voices Without Restraint
Alchemically Transmutative Symbol Decipherment
The Book as Sacred Elixir
Manger du Livre Eat The Book
The shortest distance between two points is creative distance
and Allen Ginsberg howls
"I saw the best minds of my generation destroyed by madness, starving, hysterical naked"
and Diane di Prima rants
"the only war that matters is the war against the imagination, all other wars are subsumed in it"
and Amiri Baraka chants

"They have turned, and say that I am dying. That I have thrown my life
way. They have left me alone, where there is no one, nothing, save
who I am. Not a note nor a word."
And Lawrence Ferlinghetti paints PICTURES OF THE GONE WORLD
Allen Ginsberg Diane di Prima Amiri Baraka
Lawrence Ferlinghetti
Numinous howls and rants and chants and paintings
and years of tears come fiercely flowing streaming
all the pain wells up
years of failure of not being enough for anyone
years of wandering lost on the outside
Outlaw
being told "you ain't shit you don't fit what the
fuck you doin here? all you've done is create pain and sorrow wouldn't you be
better off dead?"
Turning away from walking away from disappearing from
Authorities the past
The Dead
in the hermetic corridors of authority The Dead
somberly splash in their shallow sewers
devouring and regurgitating themselves
and with tears in my eyes
a snarl on my lips
and peace in my heart
I'm failing as no others dare fail

and I'm in the gap between thought and image
how'd I get here after all the years of not being self
after all the years of being Other
of floating out of my body on the ceiling
watching skin blood bones nerves
going through the motions
believing in space and time
without realizing I was already Out
out of sync beyond chaos
breathing rhythms at the ending of time
and now here in the gap between thought and image
where the only distance is creative distance
Here Now at The Ending of Time
I focus all three eyes in wolf fashion

Closing Time
I walk through the stone called lump of fat
and I float through the fire that is central
and I enter the upper chamber of the golden pyramid
the confluence of all streams
polyglot commingling of all voices
Thalass feeds herself
and as I float over the open sarcophagus
I am
The Ocean of Consciousness

Knut Hamsun, progenitor of modernism, recipient of the 1920 Nobel Prize for Literature, in his 1890 essay, "On The Unconcscious Life of The Mind," said "We would experience a little of the secret movements which are made unnoticed in the remote places of the soul, the capricious disorder of perceptions, the delicate life of fantasy held under the magnifying glass, the wanderings of these thoughts and feelings out of the blue: motionless, trackless journeys with the brain and heart, strange activities of the nerves, the whispering of the blood, the pleading of the bone, the entire unconscious life of the mind."

So what, so what is the ocean of consciousness?

"The only war that matters is the war against the imagination, all other wars are subsumed in it."
-Diane di Prima

The psychic makeup of creative persons attracts attention, but the actual artistic achievement is the bedrock of inquiry when it is directed toward understanding the artist, for the artistic disposition adheres to a charisma that attaches to the 'office' and has collective aspects.

"To be an artist is to fail, as no other dare fail."
-Samuel Beckett

Today Specialization is sold on every corner, fed in every home, brainwashed into every student, every young person. We are told that the only way to succeed, here at the beginning of the 21st Century is to put all our time, energy, learning, and focus into one area, one field, one specialty (math, science, computer technology, business). If we don't we will fail. We are subtly and forcefully, implicitly and explicitly, encouraged to deny the rest of who we are, our total self, selves, our holistic being. The postmodern brave new world resides inside the computer via The Web with only faint peripheral recognition to the person, the individual (and by extension the real global community), the real human being operating the machine. The idea of and belief in specialization as the only path, only possibility, has sped up the fragmentation, the alienation which began to grow rapidly within the individual, radically reshaping culture, a century ago with the birth of those Machiavellian revolutions in technology, industry, and war. And with the growing fracturing fragmentation and alienation comes the path - anger, fear, anxiety, angst, ennui, nihilism, depression, despair - that, for the person of action, leads to suicide. Unless, through our paradoxical leap of creative faith we engage ourselves in the belief, which can become a life mission, that regardless of the consequences, we can, through our engagement, our actions, our loving life work, make the world a better, safer, friendlier place in which to live. Sound naive? What does this have to do with Voices Without Restraint? With The Beat Generation, The Voice that, though trembling, speaks out against The Powers That Be, what place does this Outsider Poet Voice have in the real violent world in which we are immersed? Are we too desensitized to the violence, to the fact that in the past Century alone we have murdered over 160 million people in one war after another, to even think it worthwhile to consider the possibility of a less violent world? Are we too small, too insignificant to make any kind of difference? The power-mongers have control. What difference can one little individual life possibly make possibly matter?

Today the X and microserf and why generations are swollen with young people yearning to express the creative energies buried in their hearts, seeping from every pore of their beings. They ache to change to heal the world. Is it still possible? Is it too late? Is there anyone (a group? The Storm Generation?!) left to show the way to be an example? To be a guide? A mentor? James Joyce, King of Modernism, said the idea of the hero was nothing but a damn lie that the primary motivating forces are passion and compassion. As late as 1984 people were laughing at George Orwell. Today, as we finally move into an Orwellian culture of simulation life on the screen landscape, can we remember passion and compassion or has the postmodern ironic satiric deathinlifegame laugh killed both sperm and egg? Is there anywhere worth going from here? Is it any wonder that today's youth have adopted Jack Kerouac, Allen Ginsberg, William S. Burroughs, Herbert Huncke, Gregory Corso, Neal Cassady, Lawrence Ferlinghetti, Amiri Baraka, Robert Creeley, David Amram, Diane di Prima, Ed Sanders, Anne Waldman, Bob Dylan, and all the other Beat Generation and related poets, writers, artists, musicians, photographers, filmmakers as their inspirational, life-affirming antinomian ancestors? These are people who have stood and still stand up against unreasoning power/right/might, looked that power in the eyes and said NO I don't agree with you and this is why. And they have spoken these words, not for money or for fame, but out of life's deepest convictions, out of the belief that we, each one of us, no matter our skin color our economic status our political religious sexual preferences, all of us have the right to live to dream as we choose rather than as some supposed higher moral authority prescribes for us.

In the next decade The Beats will come to be recognized as the most important group of poets and writers in the history of America. The Beats have given birth to new generations to new energies which are waking to the realization that the creative imagination provides salvation from suicide, from death in life, by revealing that there are alternative paths to explore in this world alternative paths that lead away from the mundane, the superficial, away from submission to mediocrity alternative paths opening into the inspired brilliant fire called LIFE.

The hallowed doors of Academia, Academia, the bastion of conservative thought, the doors of Academia are finally creaking open (just as it took so long for them to open to James Joyce, Virginia Woolf, Samuel Beckett and all other original thinkers and expressionists) the doors are creaking open and, finally, at least a discourse on The Beats has begun.

"I am more than my physical body and as such
I can see more than the physical world."
-Robert Monroe

produce produce produce
young people of all ages
let go your fears
embrace failure
take risks
be fearless
accept responsibility for your actions
embrace failure
through failure you will know undreamed of success
Mysticus Memoria Rhythmus:
Ignis Fatuus?
weaving wisps of memory beyond the thread of time
ocean of the forgotten fleet
with mystic memory rhyme
unseen siren sing within the pilfered soul

orchestrated rhythms of wind and drum
ride the blood crest
to the heart
move with word-thoughts distant
touch the untouchable emotion womb
cordate-chord at the core
of OM

If history is the embodiment of "fear, reason, social convention, and tradition" then it becomes the duty, the responsibility, the compelling creative urge of the Nabi, the Prophet, to crack history's encrusted, iconostasic, shell releasing the dying and dead by invocation of The Word, pure thought, translated via pure energy into meaning full sound. The Prophet, whose home is in Shadow in The Holy Unholy The Sacred and The Profane Realms of The Creative Imagination, as the synaptic link between spirit and matter, creates a new, enlightened awake being awake world.

Out of the postmodern surreal chaos will evolve a structure, more vast than presently perceivable, that I call The Ocean of Consciousness. The structure is difficult to perceive because we are the structure. We are the synthesis. All streams of thought of con and unconsciousness flow to our Ocean of Consciousness, the structure that gives birth to, engulfs, encloses, creates, and expands the chaos. Where do WE, do I, my Self (all of me including my Spirit and Soul), begin and end? Do we begin? Do we end? The earth was once thought of as the center of the universe but our view, our perception, thrown out, into The Creative Imagination, like a boomerang, expanded, and is now returning and we will soon see that We, each One of Us, are the center of a vast, interconnected, perhaps infinite, universe.

My quest to reach beyond Modernism and postmodernism to The Ocean of Consciousness may be partially defined as a literary scientific alchemical mysticism in which the mysterium tremendum is alive and doing well. It is a creative, numinous attempt to reach a Fourth Kingdom beyond but encompassing the alienated and alienating realms of spirit, matter, chaos, a Fourth Kingdom wherein lies the synthesis of apparently irreconcilable differences. The journey is inward, outward, centered, liminal, in the heart, and on the edge to silence, to the immaterial, psychological, emotional, mental, spiritual self, but also simultaneously to the spoken, visual, material, the world of action. But the emphasis of the journey is inward with self soul consciousness at heart.

Knowledge, from the inception of Modernism (and through postmodernism and Chaos to The Ocean of Consciousness), is reorganized, redefined through Literature, Art, Music, and Film. The genres are changing, the canons are exploding, as is culture. The mythopoetics, the privileged sense of sight, of modern, contemporary, avant-garde poets, musicians, artists, filmmakers are examples of art forms of a society, a culture, a civilization, a world in which humanity lives not securely in cities nor innocently in the country but on the apocalyptic, simultaneous edge of a new realm of being and understanding. The mythopoet, female and male, returns to the role of prophet-seer of shaman by creating myths that resonate in the minds the hearts of readers, myths that speak with the authority of the ancient myths, myths that are gifts from the shadow.

Ron Whitehead and John Tytell

Presented by John Tytell and Ron Whitehead, with piano accompaniment by David Amram, at The New York Underground Music & Poetry Festival, November 2000, New York City

Although Jack and Neal were gone before I had a chance to meet them I did become friends with Kerouac's daughter, Jan. I visited Jack's grave with her. And I shared the stage with Neal's son, John, in Kentucky and New York City. I visited with and shared the stage with Neal's wife, Carolyn, in London, England. And I was blessed to edit, publish, share stage and page, practice hangoutology, share the acquaintance of, and become friends with Allen Ginsberg, Gregory Corso, Herbert Huncke, William S. Burroughs, Lawrence Ferlinghetti, David Amram, Diane di Prima, Amiri Baraka, Anne Waldman, Ed Sanders, Hunter S. Thompson, and other Beat Generation connected folks. I am honored by each and every encounter!

Kerouac's Daughter

Over the grave you stand gentle
smile arms outstretched open
hands welcoming Christ there
in the tomb at least his old bones
not rotting rather becoming white
light white heat like his writing
holy spirit Jack Kerouac your lost
father holy ghost wandering now
in other realms like he did on earth
he does in heaven his books and
yours published there where you
in darkest night in darkest night
comes wind weaves night violin
wolf song comes wind weaves
night violin wolf song in darkest
night in darkest night where you
steal away where you steal away
into everybody's anonymous soul

Kerouac's compassionate daughter
poet birthing the global literary
community "an unimaginable and
impossibly immaculate Reconception
the very craziest of Second Comings"

asheville august 1994

for walt whitman

right now i'm in asheville ashville
ash yes the right place the right time ashes
burned burned failed destroyed ashes
so what do i do quit give up become cinder for that
long distance never ending railroad track to nowhere?
give up?!
allen ginsberg preaches take a hand share the word
the poetry gospel coming from the gonads the solar plexus
the heart and the head yes thank you allen
for the energy for the love and my head rises a little
to watch my son dylan and my daughter rani
dancing to the b52s' love shack playing on the jukebox
in asheville and i'm lookin at the moon over the mountain
thinkin bout the kid from cheyenne
and the others from denver
and i think of denver and of dean moriarty
of neal cassady's flame gone gone gone
his naked body lying beside those
long distance never ending railroad tracks to nowhere
and i hope those kids from the west
hell i hope all of us
keep the funk
keep the flame that gnostical turpitude flame
alive
don't let the system break you don't let life break you
so that when the time comes when your time is up
you either go screamin or go with peace in your heart
into that dark night
and now somebody's playing the blues on the piano
and yeah two days ago rani and i were sitting
at ginsberg's table walt whiitman on the wall
in new york city talkin bout asheville
talkin bout the 20 grand i lost putting on that
48-hour non-stop music and poetry insomniacathon to
kickoff new york university's 50-year celebration of

the beat generation and i'm talkin with allen ginsberg
and herbert huncke and gregory corso
but like when father of slam marc smith proclaims his name
the audience responds "so what!"
and i'm thinkin bout the green mill & poetry alive
and i know few know how much work the poets do for poetry
but i know now that the reward the pay is in the experience
and suddenly i remember that the ash
in celtic and scandinavian mythology is the tree
most generally associated with magic
and yes here i am in asheville with
all these poets who somehow know
the alchemical magical power of poetry
of the word yes manger du livre
eat the word eat the book and the word will set you free
and i'm in asheville thinkin bout allen ginsberg
and what he said bout takin somebody's hand
cause we're all in this together we're pullin
we ain't pushin we're lettin it be
we ain't forcin it and i realize that a poem
like a painting or a song is only the representation
of the actual experience the real poem is the event itself
and i'm thinkin bout the national poetry slam
in asheville and out of the ash that i am i feel an energy
risin through me growin strong comin from poets
of all ages and i'm in asheville
but it don't feel like failure no more it feels
friendly it feels good it feels strong like some kind of
rebirth
into poetry
into life
it feels like
resurrection
right now
right here
in asheville

presented 8.18.94
national poetry slam
asheville north carolina

Conversations with William S. Burroughs

Naked Interview: Conversations with William S. Burroughs

By Ron Whitehead

Friday, July 12, 1996 07:03 pm

Interviews,

Transgressive

William S. Burroughs is one of the greatest writers of our times. His talent has brought him fame, and along with it, many burdens. Daily, Burroughs is swamped with fan mail, unexpected visitors and interview requests. And if that wasn't enough to keep him occupied, strange rumors have begun circulating about him. Burroughs, who rarely grants interviews, speaks with Ron Whitehead in an attempt to counter the public's false speculation about him.

"His Swiftian vision of a processed, pre-pakeaged life, of a kind of elctro-chemical totalitarianism, often evokes the black laughter of hilarious horror."
—Playboy

"Burroughs is the greatest satirical writer since Jonathan Swift."
—Jack Kerouac

"The only American writer possessed by genius."
—Norman Mailer

"Burroughs shakes the reader as a dog shakes a rat."
—Anthony Burgess

"An integrity beyond corruption...Burroughs convinces us he has seen things beyond description."
—John Updike

"One of the most dazzling magicians of our time."
—John Rechy, "The Ticket is Exploding"

"With suffering comes humility and with it in the end, wisdom."
—J. Swift

At 82, William Seward Burroughs II, El Hombre Invisible, Literary Outlaw, Commandeur de l'Ordre de Arts et des Lettres, is rapidly becoming the most respected, highly regarded writer in America, in the world.

"All at once I snapped my fingers a couple of times and laughed. Hellfire and damnation! I suddenly imagined I had discovered a new word! I sat up in bed, and said: It is not in the language, I have discovered it – Kuboaa. It has letters just like a real word, by sweet Jesus, man, you have discovered a word!…Kuboaa…of tremendous linguistic significance. The word stood out clearly in front of me in the dark."

Burroughs? No. Knut Hamsun. In 1890, with the publication of "Hunger," the first purely psychological novel(yes I'm ready to argue), Hamsun turned the literary world upside-down and spun it around. In 1959, 69 years after Hamsun's breakthrough, with the release of "Naked Lunch," William S. Burroughs, explorer in the most real mythological sense, whose search for The Word has, does and will take him anywhere outside and inside himself, did what only a small handful of "literari" have achieved in the history of writing: He forever redirected the course of literature in a way that permanently altered language, culture and seeing.

So, what the hell is Old Bull Lee up to? Retired and enjoying good health, does he rest on his arse? No. He is busy working his arts off, dreaming, seeing, reading and representing new and old visions on paper, canvas, vinyl,tape, disk, CD-Rom, your brain and mine.

Dream long and dream hard enough
You will come to know
Dreaming can make it so
—William S. Burroughs

But rumors abound: He's kept tied to his bed and forced to use a chamber pot; he still takes heroin; he moved to central America (USA) because land was cheap and he knows it's about to become beachfront property since East and West coasts will be falling into oceans any day now; he's dead; he shoots obsessed, fatal-attraction European midnight visitors with a shotgun.

Come on people. Wake up. Sober down. William Burroughs is harassed day and night by folks from around the world showing up, without invitation, notice or warning, banging on doors and windows, camping in his yard, trying to get a glimpse of the legend.

The man is 82. Let's show respect for his privacy as we do for his work, as we would expect and demand given the good fortune of being in his position. He receives requests every day for interviews, visits, readings, recordings and films. He does what he can, and

always, always in the friendliest manner. (And no, he hasn't shot or threatened anyone.)

William's latest books include "My Education: A Book of Dreams" and "Ghost of Chance." Recent audiowork includes "Naked Lunch," "X-Files CD," plus, he is now in studio recording "Junky" and enjoying it so much he may go right into "Queer."

Two historic Burroughs events are taking place this summer. The Los Angeles County Museum of Art (you can contact them at 212-857-6522) is premiering the exhibition "Ports of Entry: William S. Burroughs and the Arts" on July 16 through October 6. The event, curated by Robert Sobieszek, is the first-ever retrospective surveying Burroughs' career, with 153 works, beginning with his 1960s and early 1970s photocollages, scrapbooks, and his collaborations with Brion Gysin on photomontage "cut-ups." The exhibition will also include Burroughs' later shotgun art and recent abstract painting, and will explore how his work has influenced today's cultural landscape, resulting in the absorption of his ideas and routines into newer art, advertising and current popular culture.

The second event is The New Orleans Voices Without Restraint INSOMNIACATHON at the Contemporary Arts Center and The Howlin' Wolf Club, the largest Beat gathering of the year, where Mayor Mark Morial, James Grauerholz, Doug Brinkley, and others will speak with Burroughs over the phone. (For more information contact Ron Whitehead at 502-568-4956.)

Yes, the ticket is exploding. The walls of the literary world, the world of culture, are crumbling, and through the gaping holes strides the drawling wordslinger with an attitude, William Seward Burroughs II.

William S. Burroughs: Hello?

Ron Whitehead: William?

WSB: Yes.

Whitehead: Ron Whitehead.

WSB: Well, well, Ron Whitehead.

Whitehead: How the hell are you?

WSB: How what?

Whitehead: How are you?

WSB: Well, I'm fine, thank you.

Whitehead: As you recall, I produced your "Published in Heaven:

Remembering Jack Kerouac poster and chapbook," plus I sent you my "Calling the Toads" poem & I'm right now producing the William S. Burroughs/Sonic Youth 7" vinyl recording for our audio series.

WSB: Oh, of course, yes, yes.

Whitehead: I just received letters from Rene in Amsterdam. He says that after my reading at the Meer den Woorden Festival in Goes, Holland he started having dreams in which you and I taught him how to save the world. I'm forwarding the letters to you.

WSB: How old is he? I think I remember him. What does he look like?

Whitehead: Early 20s. Blond. Handsome. Friendly. Intelligent. Knows the history of the Beats inside out. He writes from a mental hospital in Amsterdam.

WSB: Hmm. Not sure. Perhaps.

Whitehead: Reason I'm calling is that Doug Brinkley has asked me to produce an event in New Orleans in August. It will be the largest Beat gathering of the year. RANT for the literary renaissance and The Majic Bus will present the event, called Voices Without Restraint: 48-Hour Non-Stop Music & Poetry INSOMNIACATHON. As part of the event, we'll hold a City of New Orleans Presentation Ceremony, dedicating to you the historic marker which will be erected at your Algiers home, which was made famous by Jack Kerouac in "On the Road." And we'd like to have a live phone conversation with you during the presentation.

WSB: Why certainly. Yes, yes. I'm honored.

Whitehead: Good. Just a few questions.

WSB: Fine. Shoot.

Whitehead: Why did you decide to settle in Algiers, which at that time was home to various military bases, rather than in one of the traditional bohemian neighborhoods?

WSB: Yes. Because it was a hell of a lot cheaper. Real estate there was the cheapest. I got that house for $7,000 something.

Whitehead: Any memories of different New Orleans neighborhoods you visited, music, riding the ferry?

WSB: The Quarter, strange plays…Didn't get around too much.

Whitehead: The New Orleans Police have come under attack recently — imagine that — for corruption. A cop hired executioners to kill a woman who signed a brutality complaint against him. Louisiana police cars have "So no one will have to fear" inscribed on their sides. Do you have any observations about the New Orleans police, about the illegal search of your home there, or the firearms they confiscated?

WSB: No. They never laid a finger on me, as far as any brutality goes. They did lead me to believe that one of them was a federal agent when he wasn't. He was a city cop. So there was an illegal search. But I didn't know it at the time. The next day, I was arrested. There was someone with me I hardly knew. He was just introduced to me. He had one joint on him. He'd thrown out larger amounts but still had one, and they found it right away. Then the next day they went in and took my car and I never got it back, though I wasn't convicted of anything. See, they can confiscate your property even though you're not convicted of anything. And that's really scary sinister.

Whitehead: Both our political parties are looking like a bird with two right wings.

WSB: Exactly.

Whitehead: The police are gaining more powers daily as our personal freedoms are disappearing.

WSB: See, that's what I say. The whole drug war is nothing but a pretext to increase police power and personnel, and that, of course, is dead wrong. So many created imagined drug offenses.

Whitehead: New Orleans has North America's largest magic community. In recent years you've spoken bluntly about your interest in magic. In New Orleans did you encounter magic in any form?

WSB: No, I didn't.

Whitehead: There may be irony in having a literary marker commemorate your Algiers home, a place where you lived briefly, perhaps unhappily. Did you produce any writing there?

WSB: Oh yes, quite a bit. And I wouldn't say I was particularly unhappy there.

Whitehead: So it wasn't all that bad?

WSB: No, it wasn't. Not at all.

Whitehead: Jack Kerouac devoted a large section of "On the Road," on the New Orleans visit.

WSB: Oh well, Kerouac was writing fiction. What he did when he wrote about me...he made me out with Russian Countesses and Swiss accounts and other things I didn't have or didn't happen and so on. Yet…some truth, some fiction.

Whitehead: You have dramatically influenced music, literature, film, art, advertising and culture in general. Are you intrigued by that influence? How did you first become conscious of other people's perception of you as icon?

WSB: Well, slowly of course. Over time. Reading the paper, magazines, journals, that sort of thing.

Whitehead: The request for interviews becomes absurd after a while. This is the first and last one I intend to do. I feel uncomfortable in the position of interviewer.

WSB: Yes, it becomes absurd because interviewers generally ask the same questions, say the same things.

Whitehead: Recently you've been barraged with interview requests, especially in relation to the deaths of Timothy Leary and Jan Kerouac.

WSB: Yes, of course I knew Leary, but barely knew, didn't really know Jan. James knew her, was friends with her, but I didn't.

Whitehead: Hunter S. Thompson, who I like so much, is, like me, from Louisville and you're from just up the road in St. Louis. I recently visited Hunter at his home in Colorado. Hunter said he thought he was a pretty good shot until he went shooting with you.

WSB: I'll put it like this: Some days you're good and some you aren't.

Whitehead: You must have been good that day. Hunter was real impressed.

WSB: Well, he gave me a great pistol.

Whitehead: Like Hunter, some people would say that you're a Southern gentleman with a world literary reputation, but both you and Hunter have escaped the Southern-writer label. Any comments?

WSB: I escaped the label because I didn't and don't write about the South.

Whitehead: Do you have a personal favorite of your own readings? I know you've been in the studio recording "Junky."

WSB: No, I don't have any special favorite.

Whitehead: Other than Brion Gysin, is there anyone you miss the most?

WSB: When you get to be my age there are more and more people you have known that you miss. Brion, Antony Balch, Ian Summerville are ones I think of right away I was quite close to.

Whitehead: Diane di Prima is underrated, underappreciated in the world. Her autobiography will be released by Viking Penguin in April '97. I hope she'll finally receive credit that's long overdue.

WSB: Yes, I hope so too.

Whitehead: You've had much to say about Samuel Beckett. Beckett's mentor, James Joyce, was an anarchist who devoted his life work to undermining and deconstructing the dominant paradigm of patriarchy in government, religion, family and literature. I'm doing research asking The Beats what influence James Joyce had, if any, on their writing. How do you feel about Joyce?

WSB: Well he's great, a very great writer. Any modern writer is bound to be influenced by Joyce. Of course, by Beckett as well.

Whitehead: I had a long conversation with Allen Ginsberg about Bob Dylan. Allen talked about his personal feelings towards Dylan and also about Dylan's work. Allen said he felt like Dylan would be re-membered long after The Beats and he added reasons why. This is a strong statement, especially coming from Allen Ginsberg. Do you have any comments on this?

WSB: No, I don't. Not in any cursory way. Of course, I've listened to and know his music and met him a couple of times, but I don't have any strong statements to make.

Whitehead: John Giorno is giving me an out-take from The Best of Bill CD box set he's producing. As part of White Fields Press' Pub-lished in Heaven series, I'm producing a 7″ vinyl recording with you on one side and Sonic Youth on the other. Lee Ranaldo has stopped by to visit you. How much are you able to keep up with music today?

WSB: Some much more than others. I've worked with and am very good friends with Patti Smith and Jim Carroll.

Whitehead: How do you feel about this historic marker?

WSB: Fine. Fine. It's an honor like the French Commandeur de l'Ordre des Arts et des Lettres. Commander of Arts and Letters. Com-mander of Arts and Letters.

CALLING THE TOADS

Hummm
Hummm
Hummm
Hummm
Hummm
Hummm

Hummm
Hummm

Calling the toads

Calling the toads
We shall come rejoicing
Calling the toads
one step out the door off the step
goin down swingin
in a peyote amphetamine benzedrine
Dream
I'm five years old I am the messenger holdin
William Burroughs' Bill Burroughs'
Old Bull Lee's hand
holdin Bill's hand on some lonely
godforsakinuppermiddleclassSt.Louisstreet
and we're hummin we're hummin
we're hummin in tones
we're hummin in tones
callin the toads
oh yeah we're callin the toads
Bill's eyes twinklin glitterin
a devilish grin crackin the corners
of his mouth and I'm lookin him

right smack in the eyes
deep in the eyes I'm readin
his heroined heart yes I'm readin his old heart
but it ain't the story I expected
as we move this way and that
raisin and lowerin out heads our voices
callin the toads
and here they come
marchin high and low from
under the steps from under
the shrooms of the front yard
from round the corner of the house

fallin from the trees
rainin down here come the toads
all sizes and shapes all swingin
and swayin and dancin that
magic Burroughs Beat
yes here come the toads singin
and swayin and swingin their hips
now standin all round us
hundreds thousands of toads
eyes bulgin tongues stickin out hard
dancin a strange happy vulgar rhythmed
dance for Burroughs and me
yes Burroughs yes Burroughs
yes Burroughs I see his heart
and I know his secret
a secret no one has discovered
til now but I'll never tell
never reveal as I witness
this sacred scene this holy ceremony
this gathering
this universal song and dance

I witness through the eyes the heart
of William S. Burroughs
King of the Toads

Calling the toads
Calling the toads
We shall come rejoicing
Calling the toads

hummmm

Searching for Jack Kerouac

visited

San Francisco

flew to Chicago

hooked up with Rob Zoschke

flew on to Oakland California

Hertz rental Mustang GT

Rob at the wheel Neal Cassady

fast

weaving thru heavy traffic

over Bay Bridge

wandered North Beach San Francisco

suitcase weighed down with heavy words

reflections upon the

50th anniversary

of Jack Kerouac's On the Road

54 contributors europe usa

front cover Lawrence Ferlinghetti

back cover Christopher Felver

Gerald Nicosia t. kilgore splake Olafur Gunnarsson

Carolyn Cassady Paul K Yuko Otomo

Ed McClanahan Steve Dalachinsky Amanda Buck

Theo Dorgan Richard Deakin Michael Dean Odin Pollock

Mike Watt Jan Pankow Rinaldo Rasa

Didi de Paris Steve Cannon Anne Waldman

Sharon Doubiago Norbert Blei John Rocco

Charlie Newman Michael Madsen Robert M. Zoschke

Dave Church Ron Whitehead Herschel Silverman

Jeremy Hogan Daniel Barth Attila Gyenis

Bruce Hodder Early Thomas Karen Eloise Teskie

Susan O'Leary Sarah Elizabeth Andy Cook

Charles Rossiter John Ventimiglia Angelica Engel

Dean McClain Frank Messina Jerry Kamstra

Casey Cyr David Amram Guy Mendes

Visions of Johanna Jessica Ballenger Greta Whitehead

Xavier Noel Christian Hansen Beth Charles Yubie Navasat

where is Jack Kerouac

in Canada Lowell New York City North Carolina

Denver San Francisco Mexico City St. Petersburg

bones white light white heat bones

Jack Kerouac's bones in

Lowell, Massachusetts

where the road begins and ends

and I'm searching

for Jack Kerouac

with Rob Zoschke

out west as west as west can be west

and still be in the olding usa

there's the Pacific Ocean

out past the Golden Gate

asian immigrants on boats

pleading waiting to get in

open spirit

the dream

of freedom of joy

"it's okay to be happy"

His Holiness

The Dalai Lama

looks deep into my eyes my soul

and says "it's okay to be happy"

what release I felt

years and years layer upon layer of

mountainous guilt fell away fell away

"it's okay to be happy"

especially out far out west

on the left coast

determined to start a new life

divorced in august four months

grief subsides anger evaporates

out west far out west

San Francisco Oakland Berkeley Mill Valley Sausalito

non-stop performances visits travels

Berkeley Berkeley Berkeley

1968 still 1969 in Berkeley

visit Rob's friend Todd Schriger

Einstein of the sacred herb

we pow wow with Todd

and Captain Jack

peace pipe opens magic realms

we cross campus to Moe's bookstore

where we're told Chris Felver will be signing

his new BEAT book

Chris Felver

the best photographer on the planet

I wrote his phone number down

in the flying Mustang GT

crossing Bay Bridge synchronicity good signs abound

BEAT BEAT BEAT

"the most beautiful book ever produced

and published on The Beat Generation"
"

In 2001, Ron Whitehead and

I made a pilgrimage to Thomas Merton's

grave to meet Father Patrick Hart. He

had with him two poems

that Jack Kerouac had contributed to Merton's journal,

Monks Pond, summer 1968..."

and on the next page Jack Kerouac

Thomas Merton

the poems the journals the grave

Brother Pat and me at Merton's grave

where I also stood with Lawrence Ferlinghetti 1993

and I'm searching

for Jack Kerouac

Moe's bookstore Berkeley

and yes in walks Chris Felver

and Joyce Johnson

and Susan and a Felver entourage including nubile neo-Beats

three young women walking their own Beat road

a joyous reunion

at Moe's bookstore

in Berkeley, California

determined to start a new life

new beginning

days and nights visiting Felver

bridges cross bays endless miles of blue water

turquoise sky islands boats birds fish prisons

San Quentin Alcatraz trust fund yuppies

homeless

the middle class is dead

Reagan Bush Clinton Bush Jr killed the middle class

democracy is dying

even on the left coast

if we fail

to reach our democratic potential

freedom and equality for all

if we fail and we're failing miserably failing

freedomed democracy will move west

continually west

go west young woman young man

the time of the grandmothers

the time of the nurturing healing feminine energy has come

patriarchy has sewn destruction

we must all female and male become

healers peace love and

understanding are not dirty weak words

peace love and understanding are essential to our survival

rather than viruses let us be healer gardeners

dwelling harmoniously with Mother Earth

and I'm searching for Jack Kerouac

"the one who'll shake the ones unshaken

the fearless one the one without bullshit"

and the sunday morning church bells chime cross the distance

I cast off the anxiety of authority of divorce of influence

and make myself new

breathing in salty sea breezes

my lungs and heart are healed

writing the heart

I have escaped my mental sanctum

where for too long I contemplated

divorce longing loss grief my complicated navel

I have finally pulled my head outta

my ass I am born again

my new church is my body

in which my soul dwells now

wherever I am I am in church

my soul my spirit my heart sing

sing songs of praise I give thanks

for each and every moment event person being

I give thanks for the pain suffering joy happiness

all and everything have brought

me to this moment

this fleeting moment

and before this line is written it

will be gone gone gone into the past

even right now lasts less than a moment

fleeting fleeting life flies by fleeting

no since klinging to what is gone

I let go all klinging all holding all grasping all striving

I kling no more

I let go all and everything I let go

release release release

I can breathe again breathe at last

last breath will arrive soon enough

I am free

searching for Jack Kerouac

Jan's lost father

their bones

white bones buried

coast to coast

ghost to ghost

I see them now holding

hands far seeing

staring at me from the other side

spirit realms Jack and Jan Kerouac

staring at me writing this poem

searching for them and I hear

Jack say

"The World really does not matter, but God has made it so,

and so it matters in God, and He Hath Aims for it,

which we cannot know without

the understanding of obedience. There is nothing to do but give praise.

This is my ethic of 'art'..."

and searching for Jack Kerouac

I realize that I don't know anything nobody knows anything

but I embrace this beautiful

terrible mystery this mysterium tremendum called life

and I declare that henceforth and forevermore

I will do nothing but surrender my will to God

and sing songs of praise of thanks of joy of happiness

even if I die in a gutter

with a bullet in my head

I'll die singing songs of praise

and with Rob Zoschke and Chris Felver and Dan Barth

and Gerald Nicosia and Steve Dalachinsky

and Todd Shriger and my sister Robin Tichenor and Annie McClanahan

I'm searching for Jack Kerouac

Moe's bookstore Berkeley Bird and Beckett Books San Francisco

Cafe Trieste Mill Valley Oakland Public Library

Cafe Greco North Beach San Francisco

non-stop performances visits travels

I bid farewell to ye oh holy

far out left coast

and searching for Jack Kerouac

on the plane I read

"...the only people that interest me are the mad ones,

the ones who are mad to live, mad to talk,

desirous of everything at the same time, the

ones that never yawn or say a commonplace thing...but

burn, burn, burn like roman candles"

and on the plane by the window

peering through the clouds

I see his face Jack's smiling face

and he whispers from the distance

he whispers

"One night in America when the sun had gone down

beginning at four of the winter afternoon in New York

by shedding a beautiful burnished gold in the air

that made dirty old buildings look like the walls

of the temple of the world...then outflying its own

shades as it raced three thousand 200 miles over raw

bulging land to the West Coast before sloping down

the Pacific, leaving the great rearguard

shroud of night to creep upon our earth,

to darken rivers, to cup the peaks

and fold the final shore in..."

and now searching for Jack Kerouac

sitting at the window of Rob Zoschke's writer's

cabin deep deep in an evergreen forest

far northern Sister Bay, Wisconsin

peninsula Lake Michigan out the back side of the cabin

Green Bay out the front

ice on the water deep snow on the ground

snow falling snow falling

drinking red wine on a cold winter's day

I'm searching yes after all these years

still searching for myself I'm folding the final shore in

still searching for the

ever elusive Jack that's right

I said Jack Jack Kerouac

I"m searching

searching searching for Jack Jack Jack Kerouac

On First Reading Jack Kerouac's
ON THE ROAD
Down and Out in Kentucky

Part VII
For Madmen Only

We'd finished our second fifth of Southern Comfort

and the mescaline was kicking in

Jimi Hendrix crosses borders threatening to ascend towards heaven

with lightning and thunder he plays

Bob Dylan's All Along The Watchtower stereo loud as it will go

here in the only underground bookstore in Kentucky

For Madmen Only

shelves and bins stocked with books and records from

City Lights and bookpeople San Francisco

Atlantis and Alligator New Orleans

teas and herbs candles and incense from mountain communes

turquoise blue Spiritual Sky

and next door in

The Store

our head shop

paraphernalia rolling papers pipes bongs roach clips

water beds posters GROW YOUR OWN

blankets and clothes from India Native American jewelry

and we're serving the new consciousness

inspired by the one and only King of The Dharma Bums
Jack Kerouac
and yes there's Lawrence Ferlinghetti
Gary Snyder Richard Brautigan Ken Kesey Neal Cassady
Allen Ginsberg William Carlos Williams William Blake
Hermann Hesse Knut Hamsun Dostoevsky Nietzsche
Bukowski Thomas Merton The Dalai Lama Gandhi
Burroughs LeRoi Jones Diane di Prima
Hunter S. Thompson Ralph Steadman
with Robert Johnson Hound Dog Taylor Howlin' Wolf
Jimi Hendrix Led Zeppelin Patti Smith
and always Bob Dylan Bob Dylan Bob Dylan
on the stereo
but we're Down and Out in Kentucky
failing like no others dare fail
and we're always on the outside outsiders outlaws
being told you don't fit you ain't shit what the fuck you doing here
and so On The Road
is where we live traveling traveling traveling
a band of gypsies
in search of IT
headed out of Kentucky cross the usa coast to coast ghost to ghost
down to Mexico determined to
keep on keeping on trucking til the wheels fall off and burn
just passing through searching searching yes after all these years
still searching for IT and yet somewhere somehow one day one
moment
at the heights of Machu Picchu we went further in traveled deeper
on the inner road we entered the third kingdom the fourth dimension
where lies the synthesis of apparently irreconcilable differences

and in the heart of The Big Bang Epiphany we discovered
that the power and the glory of IT is bound in the grace
of forgiveness of Beating Karma through love and compassion
by persevering through desperate circumstances so now
we GO GO GO we Never Give Up recognizing Now that
The Road that Jack Kerouac's Road that our Road
always leads On so Further we GO

I've Got the Talkin' with Jim Carroll about Basketball & Poetry

@ Heine Bros October 1994 Sweet Soul Blues

"I think of poetry and how I see it as just a raw block of stone ready to be shaped,
that way words are never a horrible limit to me, just tools to shape."
B *Jim Carroll, from The Basketball Diaries*

It's October 1994 and I'm sitting in the newly opened Heine Bros
on Longest Avenue and Bardstown Road in Louisville Kentucky
talkin' with Jim Carroll about basketball and poetry
I brought Jim to town to be our Featured Poet at Insomniacathon 1994
the 48-hour non-stop Music & Poetry event featuring
50 bands and 75 poets madness sheer beautiful poetry & music madness
and a new coffee shop Heine Bros had opened in the heart
of The Highlands in the heart of Louisville's bohemian arts community
Jim Carroll was the first of many famous and infamous
poets musicians artists writers and filmmakers
I've taken to Heine Bros to talk about poetry and music and life
So Jim and I are fast talkin' bout basketball and poetry and music
and he tells me the story of how Patti Smith talked him into
performing songs and music with her then forming his own band
and he tells me about being the only white kid
on the New York City All-Star basketball team
and about his life with drugs
and poetry
and his experiences with Andy Warhol & Allen Ginsberg & Jack Kerouac
and about the movie they're gonna make about his Basketball Diaries book
and he's talkin' loud with that strange Jim Carroll accent
and I realize what a gift this conversation is

right here right now
in Heine Bros October 1994
Longest Avenue and Bardstown Road
and in a flash my entire life streams through my mind's eye
and fills my heart to overflowing with joy and sorrow
and I hold back the tears of gratitude
realizing that each and every moment of my life
has been is and will forever be
poetry

The Sad Broke Down Jack Kerouac Orlando Blues

I've gotta bad case of the Jack Kerouac

Sad broke down Orlando Blues

Tick tick click clack clickity clack clack

In December 1956 The King of The Beats

Jack I said Jack Kerouac

Arrived by bus

In the backroom here

At 1418 Clouser Avenue Orlando Florida

Jack Kerouac's typewriter

Click clack tickety clackety clacked

At a frenetic unrolling vast fast pace

In 2 weeks non-stop day and night

1957 following On the Road

Kerouac hammered out The Dharma Bums

On the Road and The Dharma Bums birthed

The Rucksack Backpack Freewheelin' Wanderer Generation

And here I am in front of Jack Kerouac's old home

Where he lived on and off for five years

Where he wrote "Orlando Blues"

Orlando where he could retreat from his sudden fame

Lonely forever lonely he wrote Lawrence Ferlinghetti asking

"On your trip to Taos and New Orleans

Why not come to Orlando also

And dig crazy Florida

Scene of spotless clean highways

And fantastic supermarkets and Cape Canaveral?"

But Ferlinghetti declined

And although Ferlinghetti couldn't make it

Here I stand in front of Jack Kerouac's old bungalow

At 1418 Clouser Avenue in Orlando

Searching for Jack's Holy Ghost

I feel his spirit dancing whirling dervish words

Drinking whiskey and popping pills weaving magic

On that old manual clickety clack clack typewriter

And now I hear Jack singing

A beautiful tenor coming from that back room

On this Saturday February 10th 2018 afternoon

Yeah Jack's still singing the Orlando Blues

Sing Jack keep singing the blues

Your songs keep us alive

Keep us on the road

Forever searching for IT

Keep singing Jack keep singing cause

I've gotta bad bad bad case of

The Jack Kerouac sad broke down Orlando blues

and in this final moment

and in this final moment

having stood in the shadows for too long

we step out and now we stand on the brink

on the edge

at the ending of time

time was time is time will be no more

and it's the big bang epiphany

in the gap between thought and image

voices streams racing

whispering through our blood

rambling through our bones

strange activities of our nerves

the unconscious creative life of our minds

a tetrameter of iambs marching shouting

voices without restraint

alchemically transmutative symbol decipherment

the book as sacred elixir

manger du livre eat the book

and the words will set you free

the shortest distance between two points is creative distance

and allen ginsberg howls

"i saw the best minds of my generation destroyed by madness,

starving, hysterical naked"

and diane di prima rants

"the only war that matters is the war against the imagination,

all other wars are subsumed in it"

and amiri baraka chants

"they have turned, and say that i am dying, that i have thrown

my life away. they have left me alone, where there is no one,

nothing, save who i am, not a note nor a word."

and lawrence ferlinghetti paints pictures of the gone world

allen ginsberg diane di prima amiri baraka

lawrence ferlinghetti

numinous howls and rants and chants and paintings

and years of tears come fiercely flowing streaming

all the pain wells up

years of failure of not being enough for anyone

years of wandering lost on the outside

outlaw

being told "you ain't shit you don't fit what the fuck

you doin here? all you've done is create pain and sorrow

wouldn't you be better off dead?"

turning away from walking away from disappearing from

authorities the past

the dead

in the hermetic corridors of authority of power

the dead somberly splash in their shallow sewers

devouring and regurgitating themselves

and with tears in our eyes a snarl on our lips

and peace in our hearts

we're failing as no others dare fail

and we're in the gap between thought and image

how'd we get here after all the years of not being self

after all the years of being other

of floating out of our bodies on the ceiling

watching skin blood bones nerves

going through the motions believing

in space and time without realizing

we were already out out of sync

beyond chaos

breathing rhythms at the ending of time

and now here in the gap between thought and image

where the only distance is creative distance

here now at the ending of time

we focus all three eyes in wolf fashion

closing time

we walk through the stone called lump of fat

and we float through the fire that is central

and we enter the upper chamber of the golden pyramid

the confluence of all streams

polyglot commingling of all voices

thalass feeds herself

and in this final moment

and as we levitate over the open sarcophagus
we arethe ocean of consciousness

Shootin' up Poetry in New Orleans

Near the levee, a maroon Hudson sedan

driven by Neal Cassady pulls up to a dilapidated old house

with tall grass and weeping willows in the yard.

It's 509 Wagner Street, Algiers, the home of William S. Burroughs.

Neal, Jack Kerouac, Al Hinkle, and LuAnne Henderson

arrive, from the road, to spend a few days with Burroughs.

Burroughs rarely goes out, except to make his connection.

He invites Kerouac to try his "orgone accumulator."

Burroughs says, "Sit inside, and you'll absorb life-principle atoms

right out of the atmosphere." He attempts to convince Kerouac

into abandoning his road trip with Cassady.

Years later I'm in New Orleans

standing outside The Howlin' Wolf Club. I'm here to produce

yet another Beat Generation spirited 48-hour non-stop

music and poetry INSOMNIACATHON and I've been burning up the road

day and night with no end in sight. I'm feelin' burnt out, tired to the bone.

So I'm searchin' for a fix of poetry to shoot into my blood

to rejuvenate my spirit. I'm calling on Bill Burroughs

and Jack Kerouac and Neal Cassady. But I haven't found my

orgone accumulator, my new poetry, yet and my head

is hangin' so low it's draggin' the ground. I've known nothin'

but failure lately. And I've been burnin' the candle at both ends so long

there's nothin' left of me but smoke and ashes.

So I'm wonderin' if the time has finally arrived for me to become cinder

for that long distance never endin' railroad track to nowhere.

My spirit screams out for help and in a flash I hear

Allen Ginsberg whisper "Take a hand. Share the word."

And out of the blue the poetry gospel starts flowin'

through my groin and my gut and my heart and my head.

And my oh my I jump and shout and sing. Yes, right in front of

The Howlin' Wolf Club. I'm grabbed hold of by the poetry spirit.

And now someone's singin' and bangin' on a piano.

So I open the door and peek in and lo and behold

there's Dr. John doing double-note crossovers

and over and unders. He's doin' his oola-mala-wala.

He's playin' and speakin' in tongues right here

in the middle of the holy New Orleans' afternoon.

And out of the blue I find the poetry I've been lookin' for.

I look up and there's the full moon smilin' at me

from over the Mississippi River and I think of Algiers

and Bill Burroughs and Jack Kerouac and Neal Cassady

and I think of Neal's flame gone gone gone.

His naked body lying beside those

long distance never endin' railroad tracks to nowhere.

And I hope all the poets and musicians

performin' at this 48-hour non-stop

music and poetry INSOMNIACATHON

hell I hope all of us

keep the funk

keep that fuck you flame alive.

Don't let the system break you.

Don't let life break you.

And I hear Dr. John playin' that piano

and singin' his boogie woogie end of the world blues.

And in that moment I know my reward

is in the experience of poetry.

And right here right now I'm in New Orleans

with all these poets and musicians who somehow know

the magical power of poetry.

The word sets us free.

And I think about Allen Ginsberg

and what he said about takin' somebody's hand

cause we're all in this together.

We're pullin'. We ain't pushin'.

We're lettin' it be.

We realize that when one of us is lifted up

we're all lifted up.

And I realize that Poetry is Life

and Life is Poetry.

And I feel an energy risin' through me

growin' strong comin' from poets and musicians of all ages.

And I don't feel like failure anymore.

I feel good. I feel strong.

I feel reborn into Poetry, into Life.

And it feels like resurrection, rebirth.

Rebirth into poetry.

Right here. Right now.

Shootin' up poetry in New Orleans

Photos From The Under- ground

*****Index of Photos Found in the Back of the Book!

JAN KEROUAC

Natasha

Ash—the bleak white brightness
Obtains the sense
To flights of human memories past
A whiff from jungle's

Dark moss-nursery
Soft within black houses
Cushioned in anxious rut
My frail bell finished fire

Returned to ruin forest soil
Beneath the banana palm
Wrapped in Northern light
Her ankles pinkly crossed

Awaiting the birds dreams
Lapse of nightless seed
Loveliest hemanicula
Entwined in burly cemetery

Sleeps unblinking through
The mad Mexican night
Of deep howling choruses
In the land of Scorpio

Then also hear the rustling
Friend—eclipse the horrid streets
Luckily, swift brittle fingers
Of cackling gentleness, oh the steps

Who brought messages of love
On winds of disembodied Maya
Re-tune—through that odd serene
Rainbow dove whole

She was yet unborn?
Native streams, tracking pound
Cloth up inside at suppose's edge
And moment wrapt at move

New ruins pour down—tilt
Myriad mammoth leaves
In countries dirt, tiny
Tropic of terrestrial love

Meal blood and milk
Which empty down to fray of sharks
Circle round shine of rocks
Under moss of bobbing flirt

As spiders watch and stanchs their
The waltz of scorpions
"Let goldspies arts braves!"
What Alchemy!

It visits the Aztec sands with
Pineapple pleasures and sensuous tears
And from the wrinkled license
Such friends unfold...

Available as a Poetry Poster broad-side
White Fields Press
1305 Lexington Road
Louisville, Kentucky 40204, USA

Editors: Kay Whitehead and Scott Ebbing
Assistant: Tom

White
Fields
Press

Lawrence Ferlinghetti

A Buddha in the Woodpile

If there had been only
one Buddhist in the woodpile
In Waco Texas
to teach us how to sit still
one saffron Buddhist in the back rooms
just one Tibetan lama
just one Taoist
just one Zen
just one Thomas Merton Trappist
just one saint in the wilderness
of Waco USA
If there had been only one
calm little Gandhi
in a white sheet or sari
one not-so-silent partner
who at the last moment shouted Wait?
If there had been just one
majority of one
in the lotus position
in the inner sanctum
who bowed his shaved head to the
Chief of All Police
and raised his hands in a jnvdra
and chanted the Great Paramita Sutra
the Diamond Sutra
the Lotus Sutra
If there had somehow been
just one Gandhian spinner
with Brian Wilson at the gates
of the White House,
at the Gates of Eden
then it wouldn't have been
Vietnam once again
and its "One two three four
Who're we wasin' for"
If one single ray of the light
of the Dalai Lama

when he visited this land
had penetrated somehow
the Land of the Brave
where the lion never
lies down with the lamb
But not a glimmer got through
The Security screened it out
screened out the Buddha
and his not-so-crazy wisdom
If only in the land of Sam Houston
if only in the land of the Alamo
if only in Waco land USA
if only in Reno
if only on CNN CBS NBC
one had comprehended
one single syllable
of the Gautami Buddha
of the young Siddhartha
one single whisper of
Gandhi's spinning wheel
one lost syllable
of Martin Luther King
or of the Early Christians
or of Mother Teresa
nc Thoreau or Whitman or Allen Ginsberg
or of the billions in America tuned to them
If the inner ears of the inner sanctums
had only been half open
to any vibrations except
those of the national security state
and had only been attuned
to the sound of one hand clapping
and not one hand punching
Then that sick cult and its children
might still be breathing
the free American air
of the First Amendment

—Lawrence Ferlinghetti

"A Buddha in the Woodpile" appears in Lawrence Ferlinghetti's latest collection
These are My Rivers: New and Selected Poems, 1955-1993, © 1993 by Lawrence Ferlinghetti
Permission to reprint granted by Lawrence Ferlinghetti

the literary renaissance

White Fields Press for the literary renaissance 1994
editors Ron Whitehead and Kent Fielding
produced by Sandra Tokarz, Alyssa Ernst Sedgwick

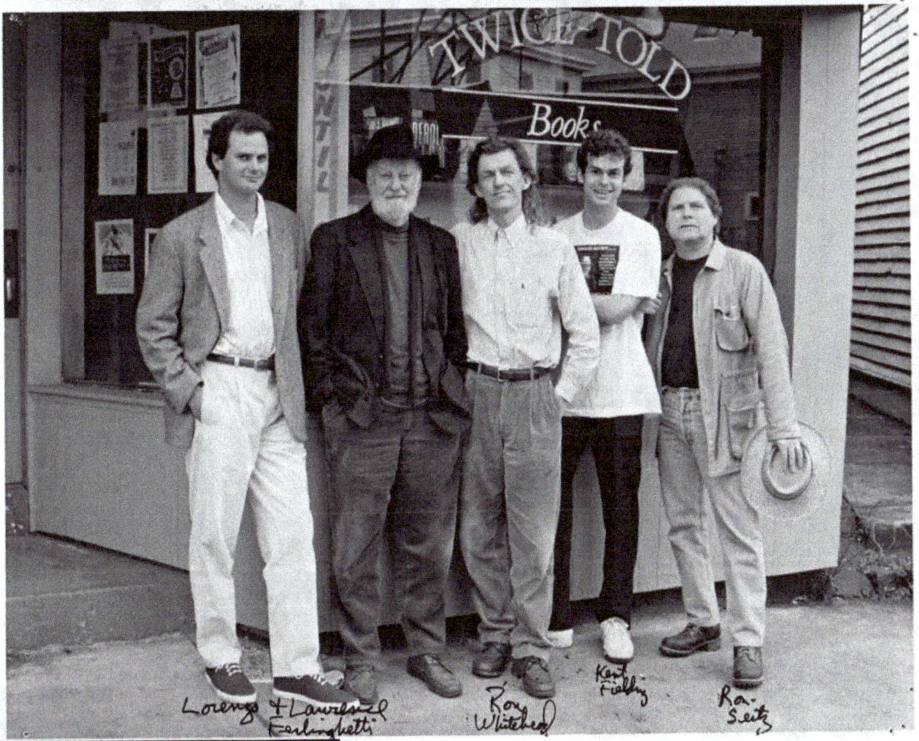

Lorenzo & Lawrence
Ferlinghetti
Ron
Whitehead
Kent
Fielding
Ron
Seitz

"I have long admired Ron Whitehead. He is as crazy as nine loons, but his poetry is a dazzling mix of folk wisdom + pure mathematics."
—Hunter S. Thompson
3/26/98

Outlaw Poet

a documentary
on Ron Whitehead

"I have long admired Ron Whitehead. He is crazy as nine loons, and his poetry is a dazzling mix of folk wisdom and pure mathematics."
- Hunter S. Thompson

Hunter & Ron watching end of Bears/Cardinals exhibition game in Hunter's Kitchen. Woody Creek, CO. 8-20-95 Bears blew field goal & lost 18-17

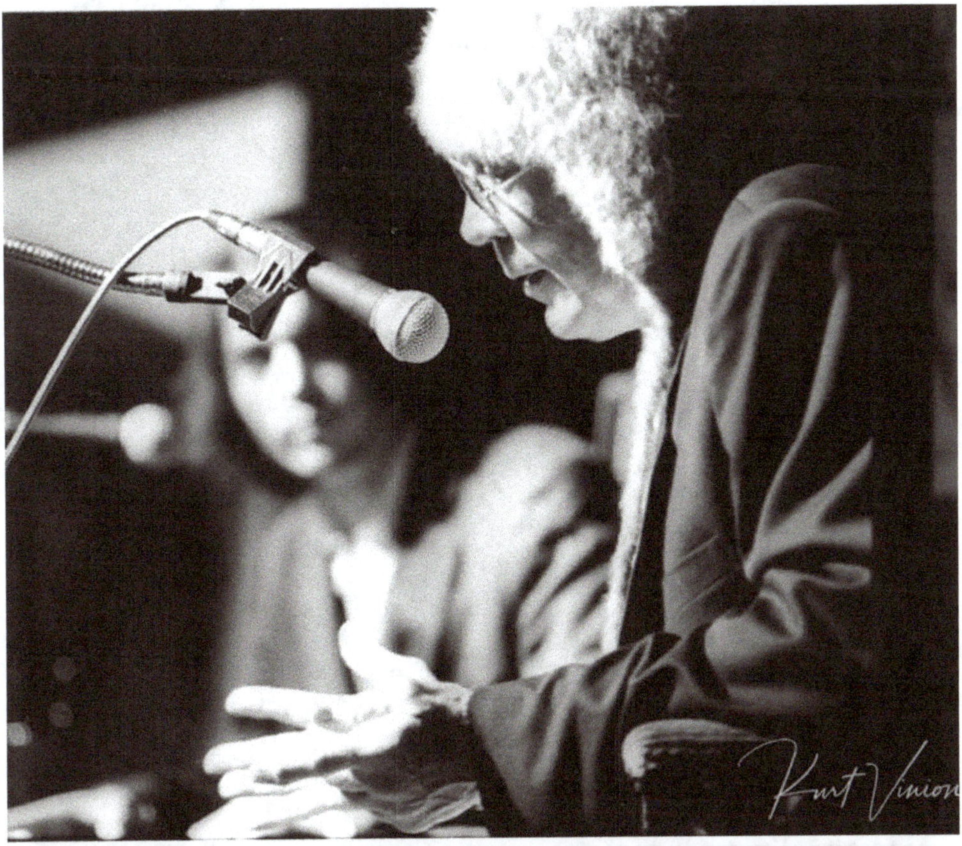
Kurt Vinion

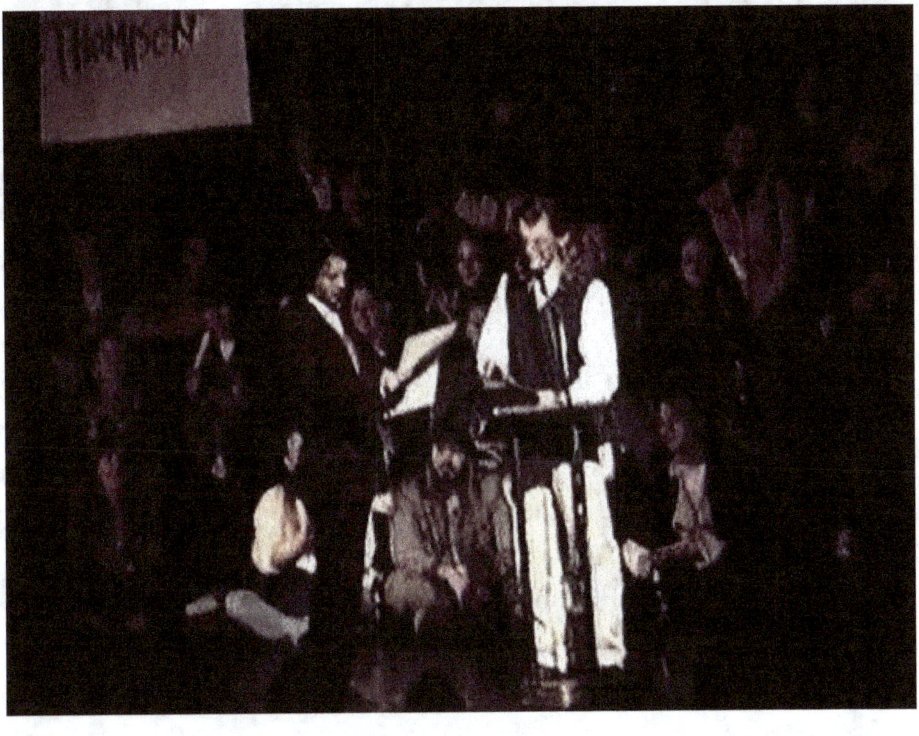

A Burroughs
Compendium
Calling the Toads

Allen Ginsberg

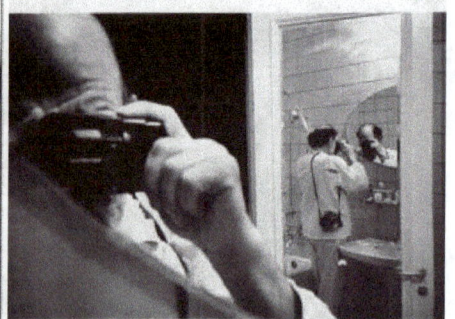

Herbert Huncke

Again–
The Hospital

Over again is the process of entering the hospital - painfully hoping nothing goes amiss and that today sends up my efforts and that by nightfall, I'll be a registered patient. Due to all probability as desperate by in need of medical care as I have ever been - physically run down and exhausted, my nerves frayed, my whole body tense and anxiety ridden, and my body covered with sores and patches of flesh germs infested and ugly skin - particularly on my face, which appears misshapen and twisted due to large splotches of infected skin which are irritated from rubbing and squeezing because there were areas where (quite possibly due to a vitamin deficiency) routine itching developed, and it became increasingly impossible to refrain from scratching and rubbing - especially when upon close inspection in front of a mirror, I discovered tiny black spots or specks littering the sections of tingling and raw flesh - and the slightest degree of pressure caused them to pop out to the surface. Also, there was - or at least seemed to be - just below the surface, a sort of network of channels containing black blood - unsightly and filthy appearing - and it became a compulsion in my mind that these channels were the breeding areas of the black creatures and that it was necessary to merely break the outer layer of skin in order to rid myself of their unwelcome presence.

This condition of the skin is not new to me - and even though in the past the results have been similar, I don't believe I have ever experienced anything to equal present conditions. Not only are the spots red and raw in appearance - as well as swollen - but where the skin has broken, there are ragged lines of thared and ruffled dry and dead grayish white skin.

I have gone many hours without sleep - and it is reasonable to believe that these sessions are not only infected, but contain torn and injured nerve ends as well.

The ordeal of having to face people while walking along the street is almost beyond endurance - and accompanied by the awareness that it is self-inflicted is so humiliating - at this point, I can only wish for death - or that by some miracle or other, I'll become invisible and pass through the crowds of people unnoticed.

Today is the third day I've spent trying to get into the hospital and if I don't make it in today, I can't even guess what I'll do to get by until tomorrow. My habit continues to make the usual demands and I've run out of people who are in a position to help me or willing to do so. Allen claims to have run out of money - and Panna has reached the end of her patience - and there is no one else I can think of.

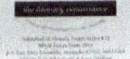

the literary renaissance

HEATHENS

HEATHENS IN EVOLUTION

AMIRI BARAKA

HEATHEN BLISS   **DEVIL WORSHIP**

To be Alive   is Heathen
& Ignorant   Self Respect
—AB 5/94

CIVIL RIGHTS BILL # 6 6 6

The Negro Heathen Enablement Act

"Essentially, it allows more Negroes to become Heathens."

AB 5/94

HEATHENS THINK FASCISM IS CIVILIZATION

AND THAT THEY ARE SUPERIOR TO HUMANS & THAT HUMANITY IS METAPHYSICAL

"CHRIST WAS NEVER IN EUROPE!"

(Kwame Touré)

HEATHEN TECHNOLOGY & MEDIA

AT LYNCHINGS HEATHENS WEAR WHITE TIE IN FORMAL HOOD & ROBE

IN THIS FRENZIED RITUAL THEY RECONFIRM THE SUPERIORITY OF THEIR CULTURE
AB 5/94

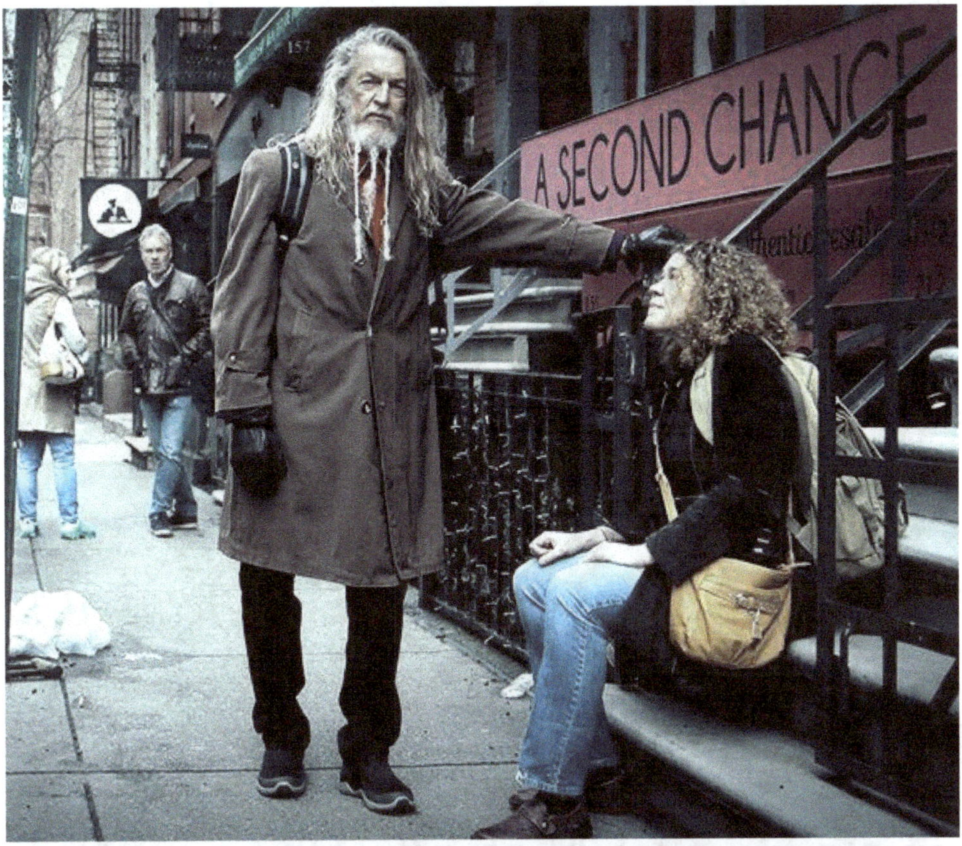
A SECOND CHANCE

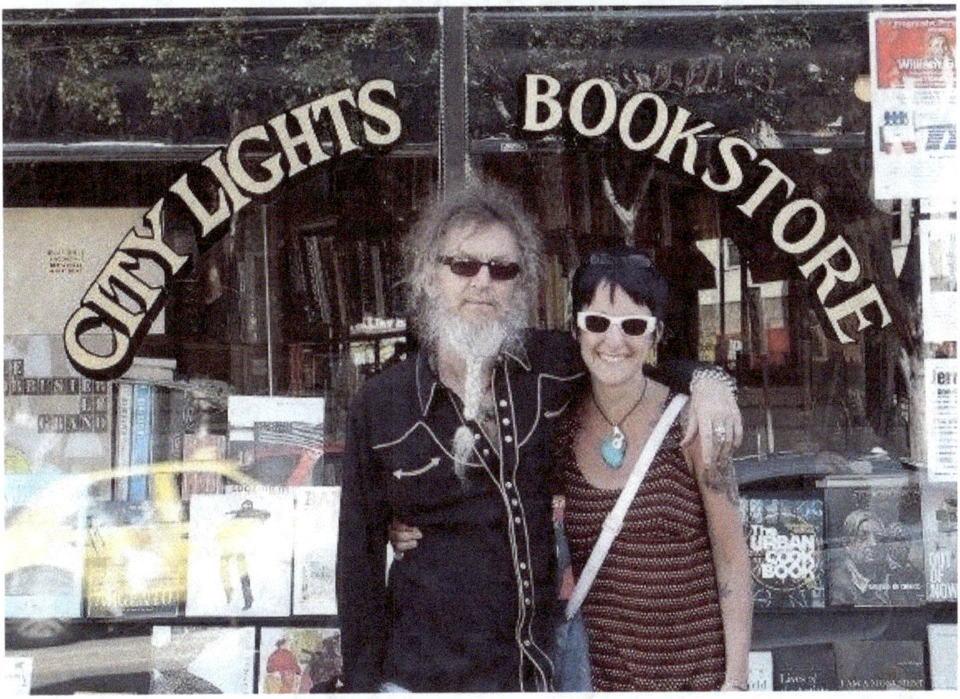
CITY LIGHTS BOOKSTORE

Part 1: Ron Whitehead interviews Lawrence Ferlinghetti

my longtime friend Lawrence Ferlinghetti was born March 24, 1919. yes he's 95 now. i got him nominated for The Nobel Prize in Literature. years ago he and i discussed me writing an in depth biography of him. i did many interviews with Lawrence before realizing i simply had way too many creative projects on my plate to devote the necessary time to researching and writing the biography he deserves. he understood. here's an interview i did with him on his 80th birthday. due to the length of the interview i'm dividing it into 3 parts. here's Part 1:

THE NEW KING OF POETRY

Lawrence Ferlinghetti Turns 80

Part 1 (of 3)

From Reykjavik to San Francisco & Beyond

In 1953 Lawrence Ferlinghetti founded the first paperback bookstore in the United States. In four and a half decades City Lights, the bookstore and publisher, has become mecca for millions, for the world's alternative voices. Ferlinghetti's A CONEY ISLAND OF THE MIND (1958) is the number one selling volume of poetry by any living Amerikan poet. On March 24, 1999 the reluctant New King of Poetry turned 80. Poet Writer Editor Publisher Scholar Organizer Ron Whitehead's conversation with the private Ferlinghetti took place from Reykjavik, Iceland to San Francisco, California.

Ron Whitehead: Lawrence, I asked you in a letter if you are interested in either

A CONEY ISLAND OF THE MIND or A FAR ROCKAWAY OF THE HEART being translated into Old Norse, into Icelandic, and being published here in

Iceland in a cooperative project with Bad Taste/Smekkleysa, the main record label, and Bjartnur, the main independent publisher.

Lawrence Ferlinghetti: Of course.

RW: Okay. I'll continue to pursue that. I've already spoken with folks here and they are interested. I'll tell them you said "okay" and I'll open the doors for them to write you and communicate directly with you about it. I'm doing the same for Lee Ranaldo and his new book.

LF: Okay.

RW: I love A FAR ROCKAWAY OF THE HEART and consider it to be not only one of your best works but a masterpiece of 20th Century poetry.

LF: Well obviously you're a genius critic.

RW: (laughter from both) I am. I am (more laughter). What are you doing now? I know you're continuing to write and paint.

LF: I'm not doing anything at the moment except lying on the bed.

RW: Okay (more laughter), do you have any new book releases planned?

LF: Well no. A FAR ROCKAWAY has just been out a year. But I now have enough poems for two books. But New Directions is saying they can't publish that fast. They want maybe one next year. One is a book called THE DIVINE BUTCHER, poems that were spoiled by humor. In other words, humor destroys sublimity in poetry. I'm getting the title from Gregory Corso who said "humor is the divine butcher." He said you can't have a sublime poem if you use a lot of humor.

RW: I don't know if I agree with that.

LF: Well I have some pretty ludicrous poems. I have a serious poem and then I put in this ludicrous image which completely destroys it but it's fun. For the other book I have between thirty and forty non-humorous poems. Well with the usual humor but nothing too devastating.

RW: I've been listening to Allen Ginsberg's HOLY SOUL JELLY ROLL: POEMS AND SONGS 1949-1993. Have you been talking with anyone about a possible CD release?

LF: This Saturday I'm going to be recording for Ryko in Francis Ford Coppola's American Zoetrope Studios which is just a block from the City Lights Bookstore.

RW: Fantastic. Just down the hill.

LF: Yes. The producer is Jim Sampas, Jim Sampas of the Sampas family and the Kerouac Estate.

RW: Yes I've met Jim.

LF: Jim is in his mid 20s I guess. He's a musician. He's coming out Saturday. We're going to record all of A CONEY ISLAND OF THE MIND.

RW: Wonderful! That's good news!

LF: He's got musicians back east he'll have on separate tracks. He's gonna blend their music with my voice tracks.

RW: I guess David Amram's going to be on some of the tracks?

LF: No, Jim and Ryko have their own musicians or group that they insisted on. I hope to do something with David Amram sooner or later.

RW: I hope so too. I'm reading an amazing 83-page text David wrote and sent to Sterling Lord and me titled "This Song's For You Jack: Collaborating With Kerouac." I've had the opportunity to read with David several times and he's a wonderful person and an incredible musician.

LF: Yes he is.

RW: You mentioned to me previously that you're working on an autobiography. How's that coming along?

LF: I've given that up for the time being. I've found that it only comes out like Samuel Beckett.

RW: (laughter) So it'll be a short autobiography.

LF: Well, rather.

RW: Part of the problem is that you've done so much.

LF: Baffling and ambiguous is the way I see it.

RW: It would have to be thousands of pages long. We've discussed the possibility of me writing a new Lawrence Ferlinghetti biography.

LF: Yeah I know. I wish you'd do it.

RW: Good. I was hoping you'd say that.

LF: But you're on the wrong end of the world there in Iceland.

RW: But I'll be in San Francisco soon. And North Carolina and New York City and France and Italy. I'm getting back on track on the biography. I'll do it. I've already started.

LF: You better hurry up. I'm 80 years old (laughter from both).

RW: I know but you're as healthy as ever.

LF: Well I work out all the time.

RW: Yeah anybody who sees your photos can tell that. Do you swim every day?

LF: I'm going to the gym in just a few minutes.

RW: In '99 and 2000 I'll be working with folks in The Netherlands, Ireland, and Iceland to produce events. What are your travel plans? I want to invite you to those events.

LF: Since I got appointed Poet Laureate of San Francisco I'm getting invited to too many places.

RW: Congratulations!

LF: I'm receiving invitations in all directions. At the moment I can go to Brazil, Argentina, Columbia, Cuba, France, Italy, Czech Republic. I can't go in all these directions at once. I went to Prague and they want me to come back and have a big art exhibition this spring but I can't. There's so much happening now I have to be here. I'm writing a regular column for THE SAN FRANCISCO CHRONICLE called "Poetry as News." So I have to be here. I may go to Italy in June and if I do I may go to Prague too but I don't think so. Not this year.

RW: I know you went to Prague last year for the Art Forum Exhibition. They celebrated you your life your work.

LF: They built a complete replica of the outside of City Lights Bookstore at their Festival. It was extraordinary. And there was a 72-hour non-stop INSOMNIACATHON reading of my poetry by every poet in town. It was held in a big church in the old town. They had an exhibition of your work and The Literary Renaissance right next to the City Lights Exhibit. Have you been to Prague?

RW: They invited me to the same event but I couldn't make it due to a prior commitment.

LF: You should go! It's fantastic!

RW: Yes. They kept all my work for their archives. I received a long letter afterwards from Karel.

LF: Yes Karel Srp. He's a great guy.

RW: He told me about how the public responded to you. He said it was like a rock concert. When they opened the doors to the Exhibition thousands of people came running straight to your table. He said you signed books all day and way into the night.

(end of Part 1. stay tuned for Part 2.)

THE NEW KING OF POETRY

Lawrence Ferlinghetti Turns 80

Part 2 (of 3)

From Reykjavik to San Francisco & Beyond

In 1953 Lawrence Ferlinghetti founded the first paperback bookstore in the United States. In four and a half decades City Lights, the bookstore and publisher, has become mecca for millions, for the world's alternative voices. Ferlinghetti's A CONEY ISLAND OF THE MIND (1958) is the number one selling volume of poetry by any living Amerikan poet. On March 24, 1999 the reluctant New King of Poetry turned 80. Poet Writer Editor Publisher Scholar Organizer Ron Whitehead's conversation with the private

Ferlinghetti took place from Reykjavik, Iceland to San

Francisco, California.

(picking up where Part 1 ended)

LF: I wrote a poem called "Rivers of Light" in the middle of the night and by God it was published the next day on the front page of the main daily paper. And it was published translated into the Czech language. That would never happen in the United States.

RW: That's amazing.

LF: It's a long poem. About two pages. So it was fantastic. The town is the most interesting city I've been in for many years. It's medieval yet it's like Paris yet it's like Florence. The castle, Kafka's castle, was the center of the Austro-Hungarian Empire and you really feel it when you go there. That's where President Havel's offices are.

RW: I understand that President Havel was recovering from surgery when you were there but he called and had his limo pick you up and take you to the castle and had his military guard give a multi-gun salute to the poet Lawrence Ferlinghetti. Shifting gears a little let's head south and talk about City Lights Italia. I know it took you years, after many requests, to give the okay for a City Lights to be opened in Europe. You finally gave Marco Cassini approval to open City Lights Italia in Florence, Italy.

LF: The first person who had the idea was Antonio Bertoli, the Director of the avante-garde theatre in Florence, Theatre Studio Scandicci. He and Marco Cassini started City Lights Italia together. There's no financial connection. They came to San Francisco. I had stayed with Antonio in Florence when I performed in his theatre. I ended up staying with him in his farmhouse in the hills above Florence and we got to be really good friends. And Marco was a small publisher in Rome.

RW: Minimum Fax Press.

LF: Yes. Now he's becoming a big publisher and he split up with Antonio. They don't see eye to eye. Like the difference between Florence and Rome. Like the difference between San Francisco and Los Angeles. Marco is very ambitious. He wants to be a big publisher. He's much more commercially minded. Antonio is a theatre director and is not at all inter-ested in commercial ambition. In fact at the City Lights Italia Bookstore in Florence they publish books, separate from Marco, under the imprint of City Lights Italia and no matter what the size of the book they charge the same amount for it. A big thick book, say 200 pages, they charge 1,500 lira. That's a little less than a dollar. If the book is 48 pages they still charge 1,500 lira. So obviously they're going broke. They publsih a lot of avant-garde Italian authors and they also publish many City Lights San Francisco authors in translation. City Lights Italia is a great cultural center. There's nothing like it in Florence or in Italy. Most of it is still back in The Renaissance. At the moment it's more of a cultural center than a bookstore cause they don't have the money to get enough books. But it is also a bookstore. It's a great meeting place. They have many wonderful events there. They've been going two and a half years now. Any time you want to read there let me know.

RW: That sounds good. I may go there in the fall.

LF: Well this year they're having a festival in I think early July. Do you have their address?

RW: So I should put letter to the attention of Antonio?

LF: Antonio Bertoli, City Lights Italia, Via San Niccolo, Florence. It's right in the center of town.

RW: What are the plans for City Lights San Francisco? I know you still take an active editorial role. I remember visiting when you were editing the new City Lights Anthology. You spend at least a couple hours each day there. Is Nancy Peters...

LF: She's the Managing Director.

RW: She's running the show?

LF: Yes. We're becoming a Foundation. We're going to be The City Lights Non-Profit Foundation. We're trying to buy the building by establishing the foundation and thereby enabling donors to buy the building for us. We've been tenants all these years.

RW: It's a historic site for people round the world.

LF: It's an old building and the owners are very old and they're ready to sell it so we're starting this foundation right now. It's happening this week.

RW: You expressed concern, and I mention this in my poem "San Fancisco May 1993" about the influx of Chinese money from Hong Kong buying out the Italians in North Beach.

LF: No I wasn't expressing concern. It was just a statement of fact.

RW: Considering that San Francisco has grown so much do you still like living there? Have you thought about moving?

LF: No the population hasn't grown. There's no room for expansion. The population in the city is still only about 750,000 but it's the outskirts, the suburbs and the outlying territory, that make it up to 3 million and that's what has grown. But the Asian population is 40% of San Francisco now. And another 30% is Hispanic. So the whites are a minority.

RW: That's interesting.

LF: Yes it's a Third World City. And our part of town, North Beach, which used to be solid Italian, is now two thirds Asian all the way to The Bay. But no I'm not going to move.

RW: You had been talking about buying a house. Are you still considering that?

LF: Yes but I can't possibly afford one here.

RW: I've read that San Francisco is the most expensive city in The States.

LF: Yes it is. You can't get a two bedroom house for under five or six hundred thousand.

RW: Wow! I'll just continue visiting San Francisco. Let's see I made $2,400 last year. Yes it's definitely out of my price range.

LF: Yes it's impossible.

RW: I've had the opportunity, which I enjoyed thoroughly, of meeting your son Lorenzo but I haven't met your daughter Julie.

LF: She's in Nashville, Tennessee now.

RW: That's what I remember you saying. Do your children have children?

LF: Julie has a three year old boy, Jonathan. And Lorenzo's wife had a boy a year ago. His name is Leonardo. Leonardo Ferlinghetti. He's a year old.

RW: Do you get to visit your kids and your grandkids often?

LF: Yes. They were here for Christmas. And I go to Bolinas, where Lorenzo lives, all the time. It's just an hour from here.

RW: John Tytell and I worked for over a year to get you nominated for the Nobel Prize in Literature. It my understanding that once you're nominated you stay in the pool of candidates indefinitely.

LF: Well they must have thousands of names.

RW: I don't know about that. You and Allen Ginsberg worked together for decades. In the eyes of thousands, perhaps millions, you and Allen were are The Kings of Poetry. I heard you say that Allen deserved to receive the Nobel and to be Poet Laureate of the USA.

LF: It's shocking that Allen never got recognized, that he never received a Pulitzer Prize in this country, and that he was never invited to be the Poet of The Library of Congress which is now called Poet Laureate. I think they were afraid of him. It's shocking that the poet who changed the poetic consciousness of several generations of writers, not just in the United States but round the globe, was never officially recognized for his life and his work. Go to Prague, Czech Republic and Italy and Germany and numerous other countries and cities all over the world and see what a huge difference he made.

RW: In the consciousness of the people.

LF: Especially among the poets.

(end of Part 2)

Part 3, the final part of Ron Whitehead's interview with Lawrence Ferlinghetti)

Ron Whitehead: Well do you have anything to say about being nominated for the Nobel or is that something you'd rather not talk about?

Lawrence Ferlinghetti: I was flabbergasted when John Tytell wrote me that you guys were nominating me. I figure that's pie in the sky.

RW: You never know. My feeling is that if anyone in the world deserves the Nobel for lifetime achievements for their poetry and for the work they've done for poetry round the that person is you.

LF: I agree with you.

RW: Good. Good.

LF: 100%!

RW: (much laughter from both) I'm glad to hear that! (laughter continues) Chris Felver's new book of photographs of you is beautiful. I've already shown it to many people.

LF: Do you have a copy in Iceland?

RW: Not right in front of me. I loaned it to the Reykjavik Arts Council. I get it back Monday before my lecture on "The Beat Generation & The Process of Writing" at the University of Iceland. Chris is sending me a copy of his documentary film, THE CONEY ISLAND OF LAWRENCE FERLINGHETTI, which Iceland's National Television is going to play. How do you feel about Chris' new book, a book full of remarkable photographs of you?

LF: Well I wrote an introduction to the book. Chris and I have been working together for thirty years. He believes in cinema verite. There are pictures in the book I'm not crazy about but he won't take them out (laughter from both). Same with his film, the documentary on me. It's cinema verite. There are no comments or voice over by himself. Just what the camera sees. And then I'm speaking too.

RW: The documentary is beautiful. The book and the documentary show sides of you that the public has never seen. A private, vulnerable, fun loving zen surrealist anarchist poet, a real human being. They are both so honest. Both engage the heart in an emotional way. I really like working with Chris. I respect and admire his work.

LF: Did you get a copy of my Poet Laureate speech?

RW: No I didn't.

LF: It's in the last issue of POETRY FLASH. It's also on the City Lights website.

RW: I'll check that out. You've become computerized.

LF: Also the articles I'm writing for THE SAN FRANCISCO CHRONICLE will be on our website. I've written two columns so far under the title "Poetry as News." The first column was on Sappho. The second one was on Kapafy. The third column, which I just wrote, is on Bertolt Brecht.

RW: Of those gone from your life who do you miss most?

LF: Everybody seems to be gone or going. People are croaking right and left. It's terrible! At my age there ain't so many left, including a lot of old girlfriends (laughter from both). They're getting picked off either by some other guy or by Mr. Death himself, the Dead Man in The Sky, The Guy With The Big Sickle. Watch out for Him. One member of The Beats is still left, and he's greater than any of them, and that's Gregory Corso. He's really The Avatar of Pure Poetry, of Pure American Lingo. Ain't nothing like Gregory. He's never derivative of anybody. Gregory is The Greatest! I became associated with The Beats by publishing them. I was not a member of the original group. I'm seven years older than Allen. The other person who is much ignored and under appreciated is Ed Sanders. Ed Sanders is a great poet. He's also a brilliant journalist. He's publishing THE WOODSTOCK JOURNAL, out of Woodstock, New York. It's a wonderful small town newspaper. Ed Sanders is very educated. He's a great wit. He's like Mark Twain. He even looks like Mark Twain. He wears white suits and he's got the Mark Twain moustache. He's really great yet greatly underestimated and ignored. Those two guys are really all that's left of The Beat Generation. Anne Waldman, who founded The Naropa Institute with Allen, is going strong but she's the younger generation really. And you're a little younger still but you're working to carry the flame forward.

RW: I consider you to be a mentor. How do you feel about the role of mentorship in human relations?

LF: (laughter) Don't follow my advice. I got divorced when I was 40 or so and I'm sorry to hear you're doing the same. Don't follow my example.

RW: A couple more questions. How many hours do you usually sleep?

LF: Oh I've been sleeping a lot lately. I sleep eight hours.

RW: Lawrence, I hope this is the beginning of many more interviews as I turn my attention to your biography.

LF: Yeah I wish you'd get with it.

RW: I will. I'll stay in touch and will let you know about the translation of your work into Icelandic. I'm sure there will be celebrations in San Francisco for your 80th Birthday!

LF: I'm going to ignore it.

RW: Ignore the big number 80?

LF: Yes ignore the big number 80. Maybe my family will have a little something.

RW: Well Happy 80th Birthday Lawrence!

LF: Thanks! Good Luck!

Searching for David Amram

visited Putnam Valley

flew to New York City LaGuardia

drove Bear Mountain West Point Peekskill

then on to The David Amram Farm

welcome to Peekskill Hollow Road Putnam Valley New York

wandered side roads main roads

lost for hours dodging deer

small suitcase weighed down with

heavy words

VIBRATIONS: A Memoir

OFFBEAT: Collaborating With Kerouac

David Amram's words his works his life

autobiography

he is spiritual intuitive psychic

"As I continued reading, I began to think that perhaps someday I

would be able to write music that might have some of the quality

that I felt in some of these writers I was beginning to admire more

and more. I also thought from what I kept hearing in my head that

my music could never take the route that composers were supposed to

follow in 1955...I loved their music, but I was from Pennsylvania, not

Vienna. I felt that if I was going to accomplish my dream, I would

somehow have to write down what I felt and what I heard and hope that

it would have enough impact to mean something to musicians who

played it and eventually to people who would hear it."

and I'm searching for David Amram

in Manitou Highland Falls Garrison Lake Monegan

New York City

"When Jack and I used to talk about his desire to find his lost

Canadian-Indian heritage, I reminded him of the Navajo Prayer of the

Twelfth Night. How the men and women prayed as they walked

on the trail of beauty. I sang him some of the old songs I had learned

from Native American musicians. Jack and I both prayed in different

languages, but the trail of beauty remained the same."

welcome to New York David Amram country

I walked New York into the wind

rivers mountains sacred

smokestacks power plants profane

and I'm searching for David Amram

the greatest composer of them all

he saves us from ourselves

and here I am in New York City

at the Casey Cyr Mike McHugh C Note Kerouac Amram Tribute

who will save us now

and I'm searching for David Amram

maybe Jack Kerouac can help

modern day prophet from Lowell Massachusetts

one of the great writers of all time

"Suddenly Dean stared into the darkness of a corner beyond the

bandstand and said, "Sal, God has arrived,"

I looked. George Shearing. And as always he leaned his blind head

on his pale hand, all ears opened like the ears of an elephant,

listening to the American sounds and mastering them for his own

English summer's-night use. Then they urged him to get up and play,

He did. He played innumerable choruses with amazing chords that

mounted higher and higher

till the sweat splashed all over the piano and everybody

listened in awe

and fright. They led him off the stand after an hour. He went

back to his dark corner, old God Shearing, and the boys said, "There

ain't nothing

left after that.""

maybe Allen Ginsberg from Paterson New Jersey

maybe Ginsberg can point the way

with his "Howl" with his generous spirit

"I'm with you in Rockland

where we hug and kiss the United States under our bedsheets

the United States that coughs all night and won't let us sleep"

maybe Gregory Corso street poet from every street

everywhere maybe Gregory Corso can help

with his brutal honesty

"O Bomb I love you

I want to kiss your clank eat your boom"

I'm searching for David Amram David Amram

and the rivers of America

Merrimack, Hudson, Delaware, Susquehanna, Ohio, Kentucky,

Mississippi, Missouri, Colorado

spray us with tears

of immigrants

who for forty days and forty nights have stood

in the fields waited on the waters outside America's door

knocking denied entry

knocking on our doors pleading "let us come in"

"let us live in your beautiful America"

and I'm searching for David Amram

walking up hills mountains The Alleghenies The Appalachians

The Rockies

bowing to gravity

leaning backward with my long hair sweeping the path

as I descend the wind and the descent flatten me

and now my muscles are green and yellow and red pain

sustaining my search

drink red wine and strong coffee

at The C Note

and I'm searching for David Amram

I want love to have its way

I want us to stand united not divided

One world One people together in peace and harmony

and as I search for David Amram

I sit in The C Note in New York City

on a hot Saturday August 21st 2004

drinking wine

who do men still drink wine

and women still water

beautiful people everywhere

and yes when I give readings round the world

I hear 3rd world voices monks and nuns

Ernesto Cardenal Nicanor Parra

Daniel Berrigan Thomas Merton

Mother Teresa

The Dalai Lama

pierce the world's terrors chanting singing praying

for love

for peace

and I'm searching for David Amram

"the one who'll shake the ones unshaken

the fearless one"

and searching for David Amram

in the New York Public Library

I look in Lawrence Ferlinghetti's yes San Francisco

Ferlinghetti who stood at Thomas Merton's grave with me

Kentucky's Abbey of Gethsemani

I look in Ferlinghetti's A CONEY ISLAND OF THE MIND and

PICTURES OF THE GONE WORLD

and I read

"Christ climbed down

from His bare tree

this year

and softly stole away into

some anonymous Mary's womb again

where in the darkest night

of everybody's anonymous soul

He awaits again

an unimaginable

and impossibly

Immaculate Reconception

the very craziest

of Second Comings."

and I'm standing at the bar at The C Note

lower east side New York City

hear of New York

on this beautiful Saturday August 21st 2004 night

and the wind whispers

welcome welcome welcome to New York to The C Note

and I'm searching searching searching for David Amram

searching for David Amram in New York New York USA

THE DECLARATION OF INDEPENDENCE THIS TIME

"Give me liberty or give me death."
- Patrick Henry -

"Congress shall make no law respecting an establishment of religion, or prohibiting the free exercise thereof; or abridging the freedom of speech, or of the press, or the right of the people peaceably to assemble, and to petition the Government for a redress of grievances."

- The Bill of Rights, 1st Amendment -

"Pray for the dead; fight like hell for the living."
- Mother Jones -

When in the course of human events
it becomes necessary for one people

to dissolve the political bonds which
have connected them with another

and to assume among the powers
of the earth the separate and equal

station to which the Laws of Nature
and of Nature's God entitle them,

a decent respect to the opinions
of humankind requires that they

declare the causes which impel
them to separation. We hold these

truths to be self-evident, that ALL
people ALL people, not just property

owners not just the wealthy not just
the military not just the power-elite,
ALL People are created equal, that they

are endowed with certain Rights,
that among these are Life, Liberty,

and the pursuit of Happiness, -
that to secure these rights,

Governments derive their powers
from the consent of the governed, -

That whenever Government becomes
destructive it is the Right of the

People to alter or to abolish it
and to institute new Government

laying its foundation on such principles
and organizing its powers in such form

as to effect the Safety and Happiness
of the people it represents. Governments

long established should not be changed
for light and transient causes; and

experience shows that humankind is
more disposed to suffer than to right themselves

by abolishing the forms to which they are
accustomed. But when a Long Train A Long Train of

abuses continues to reduce them under
Absolute Despotism it is Their Right it is

Their Duty to throw off such Government

and to provide new Guards for future

security. - Such has been our patient
sufferance and such is now the necessity

which constrains us to alter our Systems
of Government. The history of the present

U.S. Government is a history of repeated
injuries and usurpations, all having in direct

object the establishment of an absolute
Tyranny over us. To prove this, let Facts
be submitted to an Awake World:

Government has called together legislative bodies
at places unusual, uncomfortable, and distant
for the sole purpose of fatiguing us into compliance.

Government has made Judges and Legislators and
Presidents dependent on its Will alone for the tenure
of their offices, and the amount and payment of their
salaries.

Government, the largest employer in these so-called
UNITED States, continues to erect a multitude of New
Offices, and send swarms of Bureaucrats and Police to
harass us and EAT OUT our substance.

Government has kept among us, in times of peace,
Standing Armies and Larger and Larger and More and
More Violent Police Forces without our Consent.

Government has affected to render the Military and
The Police Independent of and superior to the Civil
power to the Wishes and The Will of The People.
Government has joined with The Police and The Military
to subject us to a jurisdiction foreign to our constitution,

and unacknowledged by our laws giving Assent to their
Acts of pretended Legislation:

For Quartering large bodies of armed troops and police
among us:

For protecting those same troops and police, by mock
Trials, from punishment for any Murders and Brutality
which they should commit on the inhabitants of these States:

For imposing Taxes on us without our Consent:

For depriving us in many cases of the benefits of Trial by
Jury, even if that Jury be rigged:

For trying us for pretended offences,
including running from The Police,
whether we're running from the Police or not,
For waging War against us.

Government has plundered our seas, ravaged our Coasts,
burnt our towns, and destroyed the lives of our people.

Government is at this time completing works of death,
desolation and tyranny already begun with circumstances

of Cruelty and Perfidy scarcely paralleled in the most
barbarous ages, and totally unworthy of any so-called
civilized nation.

The First discovery in determining whether a nation and
its government is civilized or not is to find out
how that nation

and its government cares for those who can't care for
themselves. Does the U.S. Government take care of
those who can't take care of themselves?

In every stage of the Oppressions We

have Petitioned for Redress in the most

humble terms: Our repeated Petitions
have been answered only by repeated

injury. A Government whose character
is thus marked by every act which may

define a Tyrant, is unfit to be the ruler
of a free people. We, therefore, the people

of the land called The United States of
America, appealing to the Supreme

Judge of the world for the rectitude of
our intentions, do solemnly publish and

declare that we are and of Right ought
to be Free and Independent; that we are

Absolved from all Allegiance to the United
States Government and that all political

connection between us and the United
States Government is and ought to be

totally dissolved and that as Free and
Independent people we have full Power

to conclude Peace, contract Alliances,
establish Commerce, aid in every conceivable

way to help HEAL THE EARTH, in ALL
aspects of its Being, including ALL

Human, Plant, and Animal Life recognizing
The interconnectedness of ALL Life and

that only through non-violent Cooperative
concerted Efforts and Open Discourse

amongst ALL Peoples can any semblance
of Peace, Justice, and Harmony ever be achieved

recognizing also that only through Tolerance and
Empathy, allowing others to live their lives according

to their traditions and desire while simultaneously
attempting to place ourselves into the other person's

shoes, imagining and feeling what life might be like
for them, and to do all other Acts and Things which

Independent People may of right do. And for the
support of this Declaration, with a firm reliance on

the protection of divine Providence, we mutually
pledge allegiance to Each Other Our Lives, Our
Fortunes and Our Sacred Honor.

King of the Underground
an interview with Ron Whitehead
~ Part 1 & 2 ~

Celebrity News ~ May 15th &

22nd 2013 ~ By Shirley Pena.

As a poet and writer, Ron Whitehead has received numerous state, national, and international awards/prizes. In 2006, Dr. John Rocco (NYC) nominated Ron for The Nobel Prize in Literature.

(Photo courtesy of Lucent Photography. Copyright 2013.)

"My life is a sand painting poem. Here gone, here gone gone gone, baby. Beautifully, meticulously, randomly, fractalledly, holistically forever. Right here, right now, presently nowheredly-gone. Sand in the sea poem poet."
-Ron Whitehead

Born on a farm in Kentucky, poet, author, orator, editor, teacher, lecturer Ron Whitehead possesses a command of the English language that is truly astounding. As a young man, Whitehead left the Kentucky farmlands in pursuit of higher learning, traveling to the University of Louisville, then later Oxford University. He quickly won renown for his gift with words, displaying dazzling talent as a poet, orator, author and editor. Whitehead has since extended his gift with words beyond writing poetry and editing literary works, spearheading the creation of a non-profit organization called the Global Literary Renaissance, whose aim is to help support literature worldwide by teaching and lecturing to students, and collaborating with musicians. Among his 28 literary works are Western Kentucky: Lost & Forgotten, Found & Remembered (with Sarah Elizabeth Burkey), The Third Testament: Three Gospels of Peace (with art by Lawrence Ferlinghetti & David Minton) and most recently, I REFUSE, I WILL NOT BOW DOWN, I WILL NEVER GIVE UP, which was just released by California's Cook Creative. In addition this Summer, Ron Whitehead will release the double CD companion to the just mentioned book being brought out by California's Cook Creative, which marks his 37th CD among his classics "Kentucky Roots", "Kentucky: poems, stories, songs", "Kentucky Blues", "From Iceland to Kentucky & Beyond", "The Shape of Water", "The Viking Hillbilly Apocalypse Revue" and "The Storm Generation Manifesto & on parting, the wilderness poems." A man of unlimited energy and possessing a true love of academia, Whitehead continues his active involvement in the academic world as an editor and a professor. Among the numerous authors whose work he has edited are Jack Kerouac, Allen Ginsberg and Lawrence Ferlinghetti. Ron has also taught at many of the world's most prestigious universities, among them: the University of Louisville, New York University, Trinity College Dublin, and The University of Iceland. Among Whitehead's current collaborative projects is an upcoming documentary film on his life and work, titled "Outlaw Poet: a Documentary on Ron Whitehead." This highly anticipated film is being directed by the exciting young director Nick Storm and will be released by Storm Generation Films. This month, Examiner had the honor of sitting down with "The King of the Underground"

Mr. Ron Whitehead, as he graciously shared his memoirs of growing up in the Kentucky farmlands, his inborn love and understanding of poetry ("From as far back as I can remember, I heard the rhythms of life of poetry") and *more*. Here is Part 1 of our two-part interview with the "Hillbilly Outlaw Poet" Ron Whitehead:

Ron, at what age did you first begin reading poetry and who was the first poet whose work you read? I started first grade when I was 5, and I was already reading. I was already working on farms, plus I started selling GRIT magazine door to door in Centertown (population 323) which was a mile and a half from our farm. I wandered through backwoods or rode my bicycle on dirt and gravel roads to get there. Through GRIT, I joined, at age 5, my first book clubs: history and biography. Although Daddy, a farmer and coal miner, dropped out of school in 9th grade, he loved poetry. He could recite all of Hiawatha and many other poems. He subscribed to Reader's Digest magazine, which included Word Power. Whenever it arrived, Daddy would yell out "Ronnie, come here" and he'd ask me to spell and give the definition of each of the ten words. From as far back as I can remember, I heard the rhythms of life of poetry. The first poems I heard? The Book of Psalms, Old Testament, the Bible. A few years ago, I wrote a book of poems titled "Kokopelli", inspired by my longtime friend David Amram's composition by the same name, my love of the legendary indigenous stories of Kokopelli and my love of The Book of Psalms. An independent press out of Calgary, Canada brought it out in a handmade edition of 250 copies. they ended up printing several editions. I gave all my copies away. I don't even have one copy to read from. Mama taught me, through her actions rather than through her words, how to give without anticipation of reciprocation.

At what age did you decide to become a poet, and was there a particular person or event that influenced that decision? I was born a poet. I've been a poet in many lifetimes. It is my calling. Poetry is the main vehicle for me to communicate, for me to uplift, inspire comfort, heal, awaken, entertain myself and whoever else has the desire and the yearning for any of the above. The influences, the mentors from the beginning of my life till now and beyond, well they are legion. I was a blessed child. I'm a blessed man. I have no complaints, only thanks. I choose to be a mentor. I've mentored thousands of young people of all ages, round the world. It is a gift to me to be able to do so.

Growing up, was there a particular poet whose work you loved best, and why? Oh my. Well, I've mentioned some already. From my earliest memories I spent half my time in nature; I'm a natural born farmboy/outdoors poet.

I spent the other half rabid-dog reading. I refuse to place limits on my reading and my writing. I read what I want to read, regardless of what anyone says. I write, using as few words as possible, what I'm inspired to write in order to create a moving, living, breathing, filmic, tangible image of whatever experience I'm birthing. I come from a long line of farmers, coal miners, "holy roller" preachers, Native Americans, Irish gypsies, strong women and intuitives, water witches, psychic,s diviners and creatives.

Today as an adult, do you have a favorite poet? I have so many favorites that I don't know where to begin. In many ways I realize, despite what anyone says, that I am or certainly strongly identify with Tiresias. I am drawn to the oracles and prophet poets: Homer and Sappho to William Blake and Walt Whitman,Charles Baudelaire, Arthur Rimbaud, W.B. Yeats, Allen Ginsberg, Jack Kerouac, Lawrence Ferlinghetti, Gregory Corso, Diane di Prima, Amiri Baraka, Bob Dylan and Jinn Fuller. Yet there are so *many many more* inspired influences who I stand in direct lineage with.

How has growing up in Kentucky influenced your poetry? I grew up in the pioneer lands of Kentucky. I was born, not tabula rasa, with an ancient history of experience. Yet I have been and I am shaped by each lifetime. I chose to be born in Kentucky. Kentucky is a land, a place like no other. One has to be strong to even be from Kentucky. I was raised by a 10th degree badass, a 10th degree smartass: Daddy. Till I was 17, I was front and center black ops boot camp. I was a master marksman by age 2. Check out the photo of me, shooting. As a boy, I learned how to kill, skin and eat animals, each of whom I had the greatest respect for. I've always felt that I have an indigenous spirit. I love animals and animals love me. I learned to fight to kill by age 12. I've told many folks 'bout this part of my upbringing. It was rough. Daddy believed and practiced "don't spare the rod." I was frequently bloodied. Thank God for Daddy, 'cause he taught me how to be strong. My will power is fierce beyond measure. Thank God for Mama. Mama represents what true Christianity is. She is love: unconditional love. She always put ointment and bandages on my bleeding wounds. Ask other Kentuckians what influence growing up in Kentucky had on them. I guarantee you we share a great deal. Ask Abraham Lincoln, Bill Monroe, The Everly Brothers, Muhammad Ali,

Hunter S. Thompson, Johnny Depp, and so many others who have Kentucky roots and who have gone on to impact whatever arena they participate in.

What qualities about your work do you think make it unique from the work of other poets? For years I wrote out of my mind, literally and figuratively. BeforeI found my voice as a poet, as a writer and as a person, I, like most writers poets and people, practiced mental masturbation. Everything started and ended with my mind. When I left home at age 17, I hated Kentucky. I never wanted to return. All I felt was rage and pain. It wasn't until I left home that I finally found the courage to come out of the closet and announce to anyone who asked me what I was going to be when I grew up, that I finally, proudly, boldly pronounced "I AM A POET!!!!!" So, in those next few liberating years-via waking and sleeping dreams-I recalled not only the pain but good memories. Interactions with nature and people began to return to me. I had an epiphany. I started journeying back to my earliest memories and recalling, even in fragments, the good experiences I had growing up in the pioneer lands of Kentucky. I started writing my experiences down; they inevitably arrived as poem gifts. Simultaneously, I recognized that my favorite poems, stories, songs and movies incorporate all of what it means to be fully human: the pain and the joy. All the senses: sex, birth, heart, soul, voice and mind. This includes the paranormal senses, which to me are as real as the physical sense. I got in touch with myself in every way. I found my voice as a poet, a writer and as a person. Oh my, this was a long journey and I'm barely touching the top of the iceberg, but at least I'm touching it. This is the period of my life-my mid 20s-when I finally began to become me. It still took years of healing,creative work. I'm still on the path of creative healing. I'm certain this journey will take forever, but there's no other journey, no other path I'd rather be on. So to answer your question: I write **all** of me. I don't allow anyone or anything, inside or outside of me, to place any limited boundaries on what the multitudinous muses bring to me. And they bring it. Oh my, they bring the gifts and I always thank them.

Photo courtesy of Lorena Wolfman. Copyright 2013.

"I am here to serve: to serve you my dear, sweet friend. To serve you: to uplift and inspire, to comfort and heal, to entertain and awaken. To serve you my dear, sweet enemy. I pray all our hearts be filled with forgiveness. The amazing grace of forgiveness washes karma away, away, away. Birthing us out of ignorance, we all be guilty of everything."-Ron Whitehead

Ron, I LOVE your work as an orator every bit as much as your poetry! To me, your finest, most shining hour as an orator was the powerful and moving introduction you gave for poet Gregory Corso, when Corso made his very first presentation in Kentucky in the 1980s.

I understand that there was a wonderful story behind that! Would you be so kind as to share that with our readers?

Thank you. I put every ounce of my entire being into everything I do, including giving introductions to luminaries such as Gregory Corso, Allen Ginsberg, Lawrence Ferlinghetti, Diane di Prima, Amiri Baraka, Robert Hunter, David Amram, Frank Messina, Bob Holman, Anne Waldman, Ed Sanders, Tuli Kupferberg, The Dalai Lama, Robert Creeley, Sigur Ros, My Morning Jacket, Blaak Heat Shujaa, Warren Zevon, Wendell Berry, Lee Ranaldo, Richard Hell, George McGovern, Hunter S. Thompson and Johnny Depp and well good Lord, this is a **long-ass** list, so that's *enough!* Onto Gregory Corso! I was driving 110 miles per hour up Bardstown Road through The Highlands: Louisville Kentucky's arts district. Allen (Ginsberg) and I had just had breakfast at Twice Told Coffee House. We stopped into Guitar Emporium to see if they had a left-handed guitar, which Allen was hoping to buy as a gift for Peter Orlovsky. I'd picked Allen up that morning at The Seelbach Hotel, where F. Scott Fitzgerald and many others have visited, then drove Allen to the spot on the banks of the Ohio River where Walt Whitman had stood, then on East Broadway passing Goodwill, Allen yelled, "Stop! Stop! I ripped my pants and I've got to get a new pair and I always shop at Goodwill!" So Allen had been telling me 'bout his love for Bob Dylan, which he knew he'd never be able to fulfill, so I slammed on my brakes so Allen could get some new pants, which I got him for $2.50. So as we came out of Guitar Emporium, I asked Allen to please check his airline lift-off time; asking him for the 3rd time that morning. He finally checked it: we had ten minutes till liftoff. That's why I was employing all my white electric lightning, protective light powers to guard us as we *flew* to the airport, passing Louisville's Mayor Jerry Abramson in limo. On the way to the airport, I was telling Allen 'bout bringing Amiri Baraka and Gregory Corso to Louisville for readings and Allen was on fire; he and David Amram being the most eloquent conversationalists I've ever been honored to practice hangoutologies with. Allen warns me, "No matter what you do, **do not** get Gregory heroin, because I have just managed to get Gregory cleaned up!" So we make to the airport with 3 minutes to run through the terminal, with Allen racing ahead twice to quickly stop, turn and take photos. We make it to his gate, just as they're pulling it. We yell "WAIT! WAIT!" and they hear us, holding it open for us. Allen gives me a big hug, a kiss on the cheek and is gone onto the "LOWELL CELEBRATES KEROUAC FESTIVAL" where he tells an audience of 300 (1,500 came to his Louisville reading, which was the largest poetry audience in Kentucky history) "Check out Ron Whitehead and what he's doing!" Oh my, word of mouth is still far and away the best advertising! I ended up working with BONO (who introduced Allen on his Ireland Tour) and thousands of others, because of Allen's preaching "The Ron Whitehead Gospel." So now back to Gregory: he wrote three new poems on his flight to Louisville, which was only the 2nd time he'd been in the south, having come 25 years earlier to Duke University. When he got off the plane we exchanged hugs, then Gregory whispered into my ear, "Ron, you'll be my hero forever if you'll line me up some heroin; but I only want *the best!*" Instantly, I heard Allen's earlier message play in my mind, as I mentally saw the Headlines in The Courier Journal: ***"Gregory Corso dies of heroin overdose! Poet Ron Whitehead provided the heroin for him!"*** I thought, "Oh, the shit has hit the fan!" So *no,* despite Gregory's growing anger at me, I didn't provide him with heroin, but I did arrange for him to have cocaine and mari-juana and other pills, plus any and all alcohol he demanded. So four nights later, at the University of Louisville's Strickler Hall, to a packed audience that was listening to a young lady singing folk songs (as the opening act for Gregory) the door in the back of the hall *slammed open and the screaming began!* It was **Gregory,** as he came marching through the hall, calling me every evil name known to the human race! All mouths in the auditorium dropped wide open, as did all eyes! The poor young lady raced off the stage to *hide,* and I said to myself, "Oh God, oh shit! What the hell?!" But being a fierce farmboy, badass warrior, I didn't bat an eye. I walked to the microphone just as Gregory mounted the stage; his cursing me with wild eyes. Foaming at the mouth, he circled me, then right before I began to introduce him he got behind my back. I knew he was gonna jump on me, so I quickly turned and forcefully grabbed his shoulders, staring hard into his wild eyes as I said: "Gregory, most of these people don't even know *who* the fuck you are, and they wouldn't be here if I hadn't asked them to come: telling them so many things about how great you are. So shut the fuck up, and go stand over to the side while I introduce you." Well, Gregory slowly shuffled, while still lingering and bristling toward me, as I then finally, thank God, praise the Lord and pass the ammunition gave the introduction for Gregory you mention. Gregory was so *blown away* by my introduc-tion that he was flabbergasted! He came out bounding like a balle-rina, and proceeded to give-and David Amram agrees with this-**the best** reading ever filmed of Gregory. After years of the film, along with films of Allen Ginsberg, Lawrence Ferlinghetti, Diane di Prima, the Official Hunter S. Thompson Tribute and and many more i produced, I'm happy and thankful to say that Nick Storm, with his Storm Generation Films, has gained access to those films and excerpts from them *will be included* in the Outlaw Poet Ron Whitehead documentary that Nick is currently producing on me. Whew. Yow! Yikes. **Thanks!**

Ron, you have countless, high profile friends all around the world, among them the Dalai Lama. Would you please tell our readers the amazing story behind your work with the Dalai Lama? It's utterly fascinating! Ok. I now need a hit of speed. Yes! Well, I'm excited to say that I'm gonna see His Holiness The Dalai Lama this weekend, May 19-21, here in Louisville, Kentucky, which is one of his only 5 visits on his 2013 USA Tour. Well oh my, this is a long story, so I'm gonna be brief. It took me a year to convince Lawrence Ferlinghetti (longtime friend I just called and sang Happy 94th Birthday to) to come give readings, talks and visit Kentucky for a week. I'm relentless. He finally said, via a phone conversation, "You aren't gonna give up, are you?" I said "No." We both laughed. He said, "Ok, if you'll take me to Thomas Merton's grave, I'll come." I said "Done!" Ferlinghetti told me something I hadn't know. Merton, a

Trappist monk and one of the most prolific writers and spiritual leaders of the 20th Century (and of all-time) had spent the last night of his life in the USA with Ferlinghetti at City Light, North Beach, San Francisco. Then Merton flew on to Asia where he attended an international ecumencial religious conference during which Merton and The Dalai Lama had three conversations that The Dalai Lama told me, and others, inspired him to become ecumenical: to accept and embrace all people of all faiths, of all beliefs. Merton was electrocuted and died after their third talk. After Ferlinghetti and I received the grand tour of The Abbey of Gethsemani an hour south of Louisville, which my longtime friend Brother Patrick Hart, who had been Merton's assistant, gave us, well on the way back to Louisville Ferlinghetti and I had a long talk (we've had many) and he encouraged me to bring The Dalai Lama to visit Merton's grave. I worked assiduously for a year to bring him. Well that's a long story, so I'll just say he came in April 1994. New York University had asked me and I'd agreed, to produce a 48-hour non-stop music and poetry Insomniacathon to kick off NYU's week long 50th year celebration of The Beat Generation which took place in May 1994. Oh my, what an incredible time that was! So when I had the blessed, gifted opportunity to finally meet His Holiness The Dalai Lama I told him about the event and that I had lined up over 300 young people of all ages, to perform at the event, plus I was gonna caravan up from Kentucky to New York, over 150 young people to perform, participate in and to practice "hangoutology." So I asked The Dalai Lama if he would please share with me a message I could then share with young people of all ages. He closed his eyes and smiled **real big**, as only The Dalai Lama can smile, then he opened his eyes and gave me a longish message. But the strangest thing was…well, if you listen to the recording of his message all I heard while he was speaking was the words for the "Never Give Up" poem I wrote. So I consider that he and I wrote the poem together, and he feels the same way. At the end of his message, he came over and stood before me. I was sitting in a chair, and I could feel his tangibly powerful, positive energies radiating from him. I felt like a child. I *was* a child. I *am* a child. We looked deep into each other's eyes. I held my right hand up to him and he held it in both his hands. He bowed, then turned and left. In 1994 I sent him in Dharamshala India, a handwritten copy of Never Give Up, and asked for him to bless it and asked for his permission to publish it, all of which he granted. The letter is in my archives at the University of Louisville. "Never Give Up" is now all over the world. The Dalai Lama has a framed poster of it hanging in his office in Dharamshala, India. He's included it in his books. It's been in National Geographic and publications around the world. I've received thousands of letters from people 'round the world, thanking me for saving their lives. I had no idea that the poem would be a daily mantra for me, saving my life many times. More often than not these days, my name is not included on the poem. My attorney has told me for years that I should trademark it; that I could be a millionaire if I did. I've always refused, saying that the poem was one of the most life changing and precious gifts I've ever been granted. It makes me feel like Johnny Appleseed. I don't care if my name is included. All I care about is that people receive the life-changing life, saving message. If I do nothing else in my life, my life will have been worth it. I'm way beyond thankful for "Never Give Up."

NEVER GIVE UP

His Holiness, The 14th Dalai Lama & Ron Whitehead

NEVER GIVE UP

by His Holiness The Dalai Lama & Ron Whitehead…

Never give up No matter what is going on Never give up

Develop the heart Too much energy in your country Is
spent developing the mind
Instead of the heart Develop the heart

Be compassionate Not just with your friends But with
everyone Be compassionate

Work for peace In your heart And in the world Work for
peace

And I say again Never give up
No matter what is going on around you Never give up…

Tribute to Hunter S. Thompson

Ron Whitehead Remembers
Dr. Hunter Shaman Thompson is dead

————————————————a tribute by Ron Whitehead

MY FRIEND AND HERO HUNTER S. THOMPSON IS DEAD. I FOL-
LOWED HIS LIFE AND WORK FROM THE RELEASE OF HELL'S
ANGELS TILL NOW. I WILL CONTINUE TO FOLLOW IT. MY
FRIEND GENE WILLIAMS AND I SOLD HUNTER'S BOOKS WE
SOLD THE FIRST ROLLING STONE MAGAZINES IN THE UNDER-
GROUND BOOKSTORE, FOR MADMEN ONLY, AND IN THE
HEADSHOP, THE STORE, WE OPERATED ON SOUTH LIME-
STONE IN LEXINGTON KENTUCKY. I NEVER DREAMED I'D
EVENTUALLY WORK WITH HUNTER AND WITH MEMBERS OF
THE BEAT GENERATION: ALLEN GINSBERG, WILLIAM S. BUR-
ROUGHS, HERBERT HUNCKE, GREGORY CORSO, LAWRENCE
FERLINGHETTI, DAVID AMRAM, DIANE DI PRIMA, AMIRI BA-
RAKA, AND OTHERS. THEIR WORKS CHANGED MY LIFE.
DREAMS DO COME TRUE.

Hunter shot himself. He is gone. He died in his kitchen in his cabin at
Owl Farm Woody Creek Colorado.

I read his Nixon obituary, "He Was A Crook," and other works to him

in that kitchen.I drank with him and we watched basketball. One night, years ago, in early May my son Nathanial and I arrived, driving 24 hours non-stop from Kentucky, just in time to watch the NBA play-offs with Hunter. Don Johnson called several times wanting us to come over. Kentuckian Rex Chapman was playing for the Phoenix Suns. The Suns were down by nine points with one minute to go in the game. I looked at Hunter and said I'll bet you that Rex will hit three threes and tie the game, that the Suns will win by one point in three overtimes. Hunter looked at me and laughed. Rex hit three threes and tied the game. But Phoenix lost in three overtimes, by one point. I got damn close. Hunter paid closer attention to me after that. We talked about life about our families about literature. Hunter was a good kind man. He was full of life. He was tough. He was a real human being. He was spirit, holy spirit, no matter what anyone says.

I HAD THE HONOR OF PRODUCING, WITH THE HELP OF DOUG-
LAS BRINKLEY AND MANY YOUNG PEOPLE AND FRIENDS, THE
HUNTER S. THOMPSON TRIBUTE AT MEMORIAL AUDITORIUM
ON 4TH STREET IN LOUISVILLE KENTUCKY IN DECEMBER
1996. WE HAD A SOLD OUT STANDING ROOM AUDIENCE OF
OVER 2,000. I BROUGHT IN HUNTER, HIS MOM VIRGINIA, HIS
SON JUAN, THE SHERIFF OF PITKIN COUNTY, JOHNNY DEPP,
WARREN ZEVON, DAVID AMRAM, DOUGLAS BRINKLEY, ROX-
ANNE PULITZER, HARVEY SLOANE, SUSI WOOD & A BLUE-
GRASS BAND, AND MANY MORE. THE MAYOR GAVE HUNTER
THE KEYS TO THE CITY. THE GOVERNOR NAMED HUNTER,
JOHNNY, WARREN, DAVID, DOUG, AND ME KENTUCKY COLO-
NELS. IT WAS A SPECTACULAR EVENT.

Hunter is one of America's one of the world's greatest writers. He
stands shoulder to shoulder with Mark Twain, John Steinbeck, Jack
Kerouac, William S. Burroughs, all five America's Best prose writers,
bar none.

Jonathan Swift, George Orwell, William S. Burroughs, and Hunter S.
Thompson are literary giants, visionaries who have much in common.

People continue to say that there will be no audience for Thompson's
work, that no one will understand or care. Yet as I travel across
America across the world working with young people, of all ages, I
witness a movement, amongst young people, away from the con

straints of non-democratic puritan totalitarian cultures. I see a new generation that recognizes the lies of the power elite, a generation that is turning to the freethinkers the freedom fighters of the 50s and 60s, recognizing honoring them as mentors.

Art is a kind of innate drive that seizes a human being and makes her or him its instrument. The artist is not simply a person acting freely, in pursuit of a merely private end, but one who allows art to realize its purposes through her or his person. Artists have moods, free will, personal aims, but as artists they are bearers of a collective human-ity, carrying and shaping the common unconscious life of the species.

I have heard more than once that Hunter S. Thompson is a madman. That oh look at what he could have done if he lived a more sane life. Nobel Prize winner Elie Wiesel, pre-eminent Jewish author, recipient of the Nobel Peace Prize, in THE TOWN BEYOND THE WALL, says: "Mad Moishe, the fat man who cries when he sings and laughs when he is silent…Moishe – I speak of the real Moishe, the one who hides behind the madman – is a great man. He is far-seeing. He sees worlds that remain inaccessible to us. His madness is only a wall, erected to protect us- us: to see what Moishe's bloodshot eyes see would be dangerous." In Jewish mysticism the prophet often bears the facade of madness. Hunter S. Thompson stands in direct lineage to the great writers and prophets. And as with the prophets of old, the message may be too painful for the masses to tolerate, to hear, to bear. They may, and usually do, condemn, even kill, the messenger. Hunter stood as long as he could. He fought a valiant fight. He was a brave yet sensitive soul. He was a sacred shaman warrior. He saw. He felt. He recorded his visions. He took alcohol and drugs to ease the pain generated by what he saw what he felt. He lived on his own terms. He died on his own terms. Did the masses kill Hunter? Did he kill himself? He found the courage to stand up against the power mongers and the masses. At least thirteen times he should have died but, miraculously, didn't. He chose to take his own life. He completed the work he came to do.

If life is a dream, as some suggest, sometimes beautiful sometimes desperate, then Hunter's work is the terrible saga of the ending of time for The American Dream. With its action set at the heart of darkness of American materialist culture, with war as perpetual background, playing on the television, Hunter S. Thompson, like the prophets of old, shows how we, through greed and powerlust, have already gone over the edge. As Jack Kerouac, through his brilliant oeuvre, breathed hope into international youth culture Thompson shows how the ruling power-elite is not about to share what it controls with idealists yearning for a world of peace love and understanding.

We must look beyond the life of the artist to the work the body of work itself. That is the measure of success. Like those who have re-examined Orwell's 1984 to find a multi-layered literary masterpiece, we must look deep into Thompson's work and find the deep multi-layered messages. His books, especially the early ones and his letters, are literary masterpieces equal to the best writing ever produced.

Knowledge, from the inception of Modernism, and through post-modernism and chaos to The Ocean of Consciousness, is reorganized, redefined through Literature, Art, Music, and Film. The genres are changing, the canons are exploding, as is culture. The mythopoetics, the privileged sense of sight, of modern, contempo-rary, avant-garde cutting edge Nabi poets, musicians, artists, film-makers are examples of art forms of a society, a culture, a civilization, a world, in which humanity lives, not securely in cities nor innocently in the country, but on the apocalyptic, simultaneous edge of a new realm of being and understanding. The mythopoet, female and male, the shaman, Hunter S. Thompson returns to the role of prophet-seet by creating myths that resonate in the minds of readers, myths that speak with the authority of the ancient myths, myths that are gifts from the shadow.

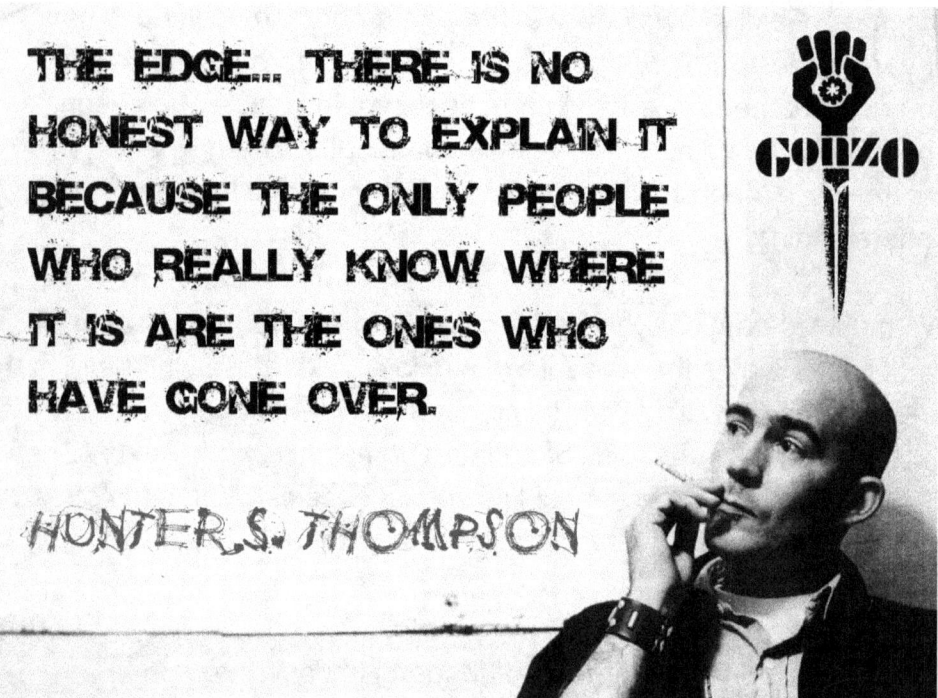

THE EDGE... THERE IS NO HONEST WAY TO EXPLAIN IT BECAUSE THE ONLY PEOPLE WHO REALLY KNOW WHERE IT IS ARE THE ONES WHO HAVE GONE OVER.

HUNTER S. THOMPSON

GONZO

The Storm Generation Manifesto

we tip our hats to the lost and the beat

we go our own way

we are the storm generation

we are the fucking storm

we are a new generation of artists

we are poets writers painters sculptors composers

photographers musicians singers dancers playwrights
filmmakers

we are creative expression

we blow away lies and injustice

we are graphic

we are honest

we tell it like it is

we are fierce

we are brutal

we are compassionate

we are gentle

we are kind

we have soft hearts

we are free

we are spirit

we are sex

we dwell in the realms of the creative imagination

we are the creative imagination

we know that the shortest distance between two points is creative distance

we pay attention to the long forgotten wisdomed voices of the forest

we vanquish the overtly materialistic greedy who intentionally destroy mountains

we honor mountains and oceans and eagles and wolves

we cherish mother earth and all her terrible beauty

we are non-violent spiritual warriors

we are lightning

we are thunder

we are songed poems

we are fearless visionary poets

we have wolf eyes

we are more than the eye of the storm

we are the fucking storm

we refuse

we will not bow down

we will never give up

we are God's open nerve

we are The Storm Generation

Ron Whitehead and Olafur Gunnarson

the hound dog taylor hunter s. thompson i gotta get outta this town blues

gimme back my wig
cause i'm thumbin a ride after midnight on
the hound dog taylor hunter s. Thompson
alligator new orleans memphis chicago 61
blues highway yes i gotta get outta this town before
somebody does me in

gimme back my wig
the blonde crew cut is the only one that'll work now cause
it's already late maybe too late in these last days final
hours of this donald trump mitch mcconnell rand paul
rush limbaugh jesse helms george bush ronald reagan
richard nixon joseph mccarthy j. edgar hoover
nsa big brother government this
christian coalition moral majority american
renaissance kkk neonazi militiaman takeover of america the
land of the free home of the brave we killed the indians
why not the decadent poets artists musicians blacks jews
hispanics asians middle easterners homo lesbians beat generation x
smart women smart women outsiders the sad downtrodden
stepped on walked on kicked and killed all the morally
depraved

yes please gimme back my wig
i don't think the red afro gonna work need that skinhead
look tonight slippin left to right and over the fence outta
this hellhole backstreet underground alley i been crowded
into by american brown shirt arm band schoolyard bully
thugs

gimme back my wig
i'm climbing out the back window paint brushes and pens
old canvases crumpled papers peanut butter sandwich
hanging from my back all my possessions as the swat
team breaks down the front door cause i'm behind on my
rent and the land lord come to pay me a visit
yes i'm convicted of being on the wrong side and i'm
convinced that this new state is taxation without
representation and i've watched this new state force the
1st amendment to disappear and i've experienced the
protection of this new omnipotent police state of by and
for the rich

yes i say it's high time

to put on my wig
and finally say
goodbye

cause i got a lethal dose of the hound dog taylor
hunter s. thompson gimme back my wig
i gotta get outta this town
blues

tapping my own phone

i'm going straight bought myself a flat top

haircut so stiff I can carry a tray of martinis

waiting on people someone to open up her

purse and give me a tip cause i don't have

a clue anymore as to what's going on but

i do know that i'm one step ahead tapping

my own phone to hear myself talking with

people who used to be my friends listening

so i can correct myself before they do and

i've got a surveillance camera in my aban-
doned

car across the street watching myself replay-
ing

the tape so i can see if i'm acting funny before

they catch me doing something i shouldn't

like yesterday i spotted myself walking too

fast and i heard myself talking too loud yes

i've got the deep fear paranoia anxiety de-
spair

and suicide blues but i'm making sure i don't

do nothing else wrong cause i done screwed

up so many times i cornered myself into a

backstreet dead end alley of paranoia and

every

time i hear an airplane or helicopter or car

door slam i know the secret service the fbi

and the irs swat teams have finally arrived

cause i published a poem by the president of

the united states of america without his

fully conscious permission and i'm sure i

haven't paid enough taxes cause i've got no

income yet somehow i keep on doing things

like eating every once in a while and paying

a light bill or two but how do i do it they're

gonna ask what's the source of your income

and how come you don't come to see us

anymore so yes i've become a little jumpy

but i'm staying one step ahead tapping my

own phone videotaping my every move

watching myself day and night replaying

the tapes cause i got a bad bad bad case

of the deep fear paranoia anxiety despair

and suicide blues

SHITHOUSE MANIFESTO

poets come out of your toilets

you've been holed up too long

playing with yourselves with

your wastes you're wasting away

all olfactory sensations dead

what with your head now situated

on your posterior one eyed cyclopian

peering down into midnight bottom

of the outhouse and it's time to

throw away the corncobs and Sears

catalogs and walk back out into

the barnyards the open pastures

of the world where animals and

people and flowers still bloom

where the sun still shines through

the moon at midnight in that other

world you've lost until now it's

high time to wake up pull your sad

face and every other hanging down

part of you out of that stinking

forlorn lost world you'll be fertilizer

soon enough for now it's time to

reconstruct who you are your life

time to check out of the amnesia

motel and get back on the highway

61 or 66 or 69 and finally say

goodbye to those lonesome lost

blue pieces of who you used to

be and say hello to this yellow

sunrise post-world where the crows

are grinning and the morning glories

sing

Death Threats, Hunter S. Thompson, Lawrence Ferlinghetti, and The Dalai Lama

In the summer of 1995

On a sizzling hot Saturday morning

I received a death threat

Written in large what looked to be blood letters

At the downtown 7th Street Post Office

Across the wall above my P.O. Box the letters said

RON WHITEHEAD WILL DIE AUGUST 20TH

My P.O.Box was full of mail including a letter from Jim Carroll

And a large hand crayon colored art package

Filled with signed books from Allen Ginsberg

The Postal Inspector and 32 police officers took photos

And interviewed me asking

"Do you have any enemies?!"

The Louisville Free Public Library Main Branch 4th & York

Was having a big exhibit of my work

Walls covered with posters

Glass cases filled with signed books and handwritten letters

On the Monday morning after the death threat

I discovered that someone had defaced

The Published in Heaven Never Give Up poster

Calling The Dalai Lama and me terrible names plus

Calling us Anti-American

Telling us to "Get The Hell Out Of America!"

For nights and nights there were phone calls

"Hello Hello Hello" click no response

For nights and nights there were

Car doors slamming tires squealing

At 2 & 3 & 4am

Mamaw died Louverine Igleheart Render

Mama's mother my grandmother

After the funeral at the Centertown Baptist Church

I loaded my family into the rental car and headed west

For a 5,000 mile 2 week road trip

We drove 24 hours non-stop

Kentucky Illinois Missouri Kansas Colorado

Pikes Peak Independence Pass Aspen Woody Creek

To Owl Farm

My kids knew about Hunter S. Thompson

My oldest son Nathanial and my daughter Rani

Had met him in NYC a year earlier

They had been 2 of the 150 young people

I took with me to attend and participate in

The 48 hour non-stop music & poetry INSOMNIACATHON

I produced to kickoff New York University's

Week long 50 year celebration of

The Beat Generation

As we pulled up in the night and passed through

The vulture protected gateway

To Hunter S. Thompson's Owl Farm front door

Loud speakers in the yard were cranked all the way up

With God awful growls and screams

Of what sounded like a bear eating a baby

Hunter offered me cocaine and marijuana and bourbon

He signed 100 copies of He Was A Crook The Nixon Obituary

Published in Heaven Poster he asked me to read it to him

We exchanged gifts long talks good time

Jack Nicholson called 3 times

Further into and through the night

Non-stop I drove to

261 Columbus Avenue North Beach

City Lights San Francisco where

We hooked up with Lawrence Ferlinghetti

He took us to the Chinese Restaurant

Down the hill after the meal

One of my kids asked for a Fortune Cookie

Which pissed the waiter off

He said "That American Not Chinese!"

Back at City Lights we hung out for hours

Lawrence gave each of us a hundred dollars worth of books

I gave him the Published in Heaven He Was A Crook Poster

Hunter signed for him plus

He bought hundreds of copies of the limited edition poster

Plus others I had brought Poemed Posters by

Allen Ginsberg and Gregory Corso and Herbert Huncke and

Lawrence Ferlinghetti and Diane di Prima and

William S. Burroughs and others

We wandered ChinaTown and Fisherman's Wharf and

and Coit Tower and Golden Gate Bridge

Where Nathanial yelled "Hey Look!"

And we turned to see him standing on the railing not

Holding on to anything the wind blowing hard

Sailboats below in the distance

I said "Get The Hell Down! Right Now!"

Damn another close call that boy has

Nerves of steel we drove through national parks

Yosemite Sequoia Painted Desert The Grand Canyon

In the night my youngest son Dylan opened his eyes

And recited the last 20 pages of John Steinbeck's

Of Mice and Men

He didn't miss a word

His eyes were glazed staring I pulled over and

Watched and listened checking referencing the book which

I lifted from his lap he had just finished reading it before he fell

Asleep as soon as he said the last word of the book he closed

His eyes and went back to sleep

Astonished I drove on into the night

Returning home to Louisville soon as we unpacked

I went to visit Hunter's mom Virginia

Hunter had asked me to keep an eye on her

Because more and more people were bothering her

Claiming to be friends of hunter trying to get inside information For unapproved biographies

So that was the beginning of my friendship with

Virginia Thompson a remarkable lady retired librarian

Who loved her bourbon she called often and invited me

To visit and at the end of each call she said

"Oh Ron please bring me some bourbon. You'll

have to sneak it in. They won't let me have it here."

So I did and first thing she'd say when I arrived was

"I promise to not talk about Hunter today!"

But after her second glass of bourbon Hunter was her

Main topic of conversation for the next several hours

And the rest of the bourbon Virginia was a delightful person

I sure saw Hunter in her

After that first visit with Virginia I went home and

Took a nap then drove 15 hours to Cambridge Massachusetts

With only enough money for gas

I couldn't find a place to piss without having to pay

So i found a spot in the middle of a parking lot

Opened the door leaned over and pissed

I didn't have money for a hotel so I slept for two hours

In my old Nissan Sentra at a gas station on the expressway

I woke up with my son Dylan and The Dalai Lama

In the back seat I was having a lucid dream

They gave me a long talk words of encouragement

Letting me know I was on the right path

To persevere then when I really woke up I drove

Back into Cambridge parked by the Charles Hotel

And walked to The Charles River

I sat on a bench at sunrise I prayed and meditated

As rowers rowed and as the sun rose

I walked to the Charles Hotel where I had been

Invited to meet The Dalai Lama

He loved the Never Give Up poem

I had written April 1994

In response to the message he gave me

The Dalai Lama took my right hand in both his hands

He looked deep into my eyes and said

"It's okay to be happy!"

The Dalai Lama bowed

Then I drove from Cambridge to Louisville

Where I took a nap took care of some business

Then drove to New York City to JFK airport

Where I boarded a plane

To amsterdam for my first performance tour

Of The Netherlands

Post Script

The Postal Inspector turned my death threat investigation

Over to The Federal Bureau of Investigation

The FBI agent interviewed me

Over the phone he said "Call back in a week."

I called back he said

"No news. Call back in a week."

I called back in a week he said

"Sorry somehow we've lost your file."

Post Post Script

His Holiness The Dalai Lama

Has the Published in Heaven

Never Give Up Poster displayed

In his private office in Dharamsala India

And I've finally realized

It is okay to be happy

Descriptions of photos

1) Natasha by Jan Kerouac, Published in Heaven Poster, WhiteFields Press.

2) A Buddha in The Woodpile by Lawrence Ferlinghetti, Published in Heaven Poster, WhiteFields Press.

3) Lorenzo Ferlinghetti, Lawrence Ferlinghetti, Ron Whitehead, Kent Fielding, Ron Seitz, standing in front of Twice Told Books, Bardstown Road, Louisville, Kentucky, April 1993, on the way to visit Thomas Merton's grave at The Abbey of Gethsemani, Trappist, Kentucky. Photo by C. Coddington.

4) Ron Whitehead with Toad Queen, after Ron performed his poem Calling The Toads with Zu Zu Ya Ya, Jimmy Can't Dance, 2019.

5) Ron Whitehead and Allen Ginsberg, Intermission book signing, Allen Ginsberg's International Reading Series performance, University of Louisville. 1,500 attended. Photo by C. Coddington.

6) Hunter S. Thompson, Ron Whitehead, Wendell Berry. Ron had just inducted Hunter S. Thompson into The Kentucky Writers Hall of Fame, followed by Wendell Berry being inducted. Photo by Jinn Bug.

7) "I have long admired Ron Whitehead. He is crazy as nine loons, and his poetry is a dazzling mix of folk wisdom and pure mathematics." Hunter S. Thompson, original handwritten message from Hunter S. Thompson, Rare Books & Archives, Ekstrom Library, University of Louisville.

8) David Amram and Ron Whitehead, KENTUCKY BOUND Concert, Jimmy Can't Dance, Louisville, Kentucky, August 2018. Photo by Jinn Bug.

9) Ron Whitehead performing with David Amram Quartet, Bowery Poetry Club, New York City. Photo by Jeremy

Hogan.

10) Hunter S. Thompson and Ron Whitehead, with gun, The Kitchen, Owl Farm, Woody Creek, Colorado, August 1995. Official poster for Outlaw Poet: A documentary on Ron Whitehead, Storm Generation Films. Photo by Deborah Fuller.

11) Hunter S. Thompson and Ron Whitehead watching the Bears/Cardinals NFL Exhibition game, The Kitchen, Owl Farm, Woody Creek, Colorado, August 20, 1995. Photo by Deborah Fuller.

12) Johnny Depp and Hunter S. Thompson, Official Hunter S. Thompson Tribute produced by Ron Whitehead, December 12, 1996, Memorial Auditorium, Louisville, Kentucky. Photo by Kurt Vinion.

13) Johnny Depp being named a Kentucky Colonel by Ron Whitehead, Official Hunter S. Thompson Tribute, December 12, 1996. From film still, bootleg footage by Tim Moorhead, for Outlaw Poet: A documentary on Ron Whitehead.

14) A Burroughs Compendium: Calling The Toads, front cover, Fringecore. Book produced by Ron Whitehead.

15) Cosmopolitan Greetings by Allen Ginsberg, Published in Heaven Posters, WhiteFields Press.

16) Lawrence Ferlinghetti and Ron Whitehead, Poetry Room, City Lights Books, San Francisco, The Viking Hillbilly Apocalypse Revue Coast to Coast Wanderer Tour.

17) Again-The Hospital by Herbert Huncke, Published in Heaven Poster, WhiteFields Press.

18) Manifesto: The Mad Farmer Liberation Front by Wendell Berry, Published in Heaven Poster, WhiteFields Press.

19) Heathens by Amiri Baraka, Published in Heaven Poster, WhiteFields Press.

20) IN SEARCH OF EROS by Lawrence Ferlinghetti, Ron Whitehead, William Plumley, Douglas Imbrogno, Published

in Heaven Chapbook, WhiteFields Press.

21) Yevgeny Yevtushenko & Ron Whitehead, Granada, Nicaragua, 2010

22) Hunter S. Thompson signing He Was A Crook: Nixon Obituary, Published in Heaven Poster, WhiteFields Press, The Kitchen, Owl Farm, Woody Creek, Colorado, August 1995. Photo by Deborah Fuller.

22) Ron Whitehead and Jinn Bug, Bleeker Street, 2017, on way to Ron's basketball book release at The Poet's House. (searching for name of photographer.)

23) Ron Whitehead and his daughter, Rani, in front of City Lights Books, San Francisco.

24) Lawrence Ferlinghetti and Ron Whitehead, at end of visit, in front of Ferlinghetti's North Beach apartment, San Francisco.

25) Interview photos have descriptions.

26) Ron Whitehead reading He Was A Crook: Nixon Obituary to Hunter S. Thompson and Ron's daughter, Rani, The Kitchen, Owl Farm, Woody Creek, Colorado, August 1995. Photo by Deborah Fuller.

27) Hunter S. Thompson and Ron Whitehead, with gun, The Kitchen, Owl Farm, Woody Creek, Colorado, August 1995. Photo by Deborah Fuller.

Bio Photo by Jinn Bug

in Heaven Chapbook, WhiteFields Press.

21) Yevgeny Yevtushenko & Ron Whitehead, Granada, Nicaragua, 2010

22) Hunter S. Thompson signing He Was A Crook: Nixon Obituary, Published in Heaven Poster, WhiteFields Press, The Kitchen, Owl Farm, Woody Creek, Colorado, August 1995. Photo by Deborah Fuller.

22) Ron Whitehead and Jinn Bug, Bleeker Street, 2017, on way to Ron's basketball book release at The Poet's House. (searching for name of photographer.)

23) Ron Whitehead and his daughter, Rani, in front of City Lights Books, San Francisco.

24) Lawrence Ferlinghetti and Ron Whitehead, at end of visit, in front of Ferlinghetti's North Beach apartment, San Francisco.

25) Interview photos have descriptions.

26) Ron Whitehead reading He Was A Crook: Nixon Obituary to Hunter S. Thompson and Ron's daughter, Rani, The Kitchen, Owl Farm, Woody Creek, Colorado, August 1995. Photo by Deborah Fuller.

27) Hunter S. Thompson and Ron Whitehead, with gun, The Kitchen, Owl Farm, Woody Creek, Colorado, August 1995. Photo by Deborah Fuller.

Bio Photo by Jinn Bug

Ron Whitehead is poet, writer, editor, publisher, organizer, scholar, professor. He grew up on a farm in Kentucky. He attended The University of Louisville and Oxford University. As a poet and writer he is the recipient of numerous state, national, and international awards/prizes including The All Kentucky Poetry Prize, The Joshua B. Everett Oxford Scholar Award, English Speaking Union Oxford Scholarship (to study at the University of Oxford's International Graduate School with Dr. Valentine Cunningham, Head of English Literature at Oxford), The Yeats Club of Oxford's Prize for Poetry. In 2006, Dr. John Rocco (NYC) nominated Ron for the Nobel Prize in Literature. In 2004, Ron was inducted into Ohio County High School's Hall of Fame, representing his 1968 graduating class. Ron's poetry has been published around the world in a diverse range of print and online publications from TRIQUARTERLY (Northwestern University/Illinois) to ARTFORUM (Czech Republic) to BLUE BEAT JACKET (Japan) to BEAT SCENE (England) to SOUTHERN REVIEW (Louisiana) to TRIBE magazine (NYC). Ron's work is held by museum, library, and private collections around the world. The University of Louisville Rare Books & Archives, directed by Delinda Buie, is the permanent repository for Ron's work (past, present, future), and several exhibits from these archives have been held, most recently at the main branch of the Louisville Free Public Library (November 2018-January 2019). Ron's poems have been translated into Spanish, Icelandic, Estonian, Portuguese, Dutch, Chinese, Japanese, French, Finnish, Tibetan, Greek, Italian, Czech, and other languages.   Ron has served as guest editor for magazines and anthologies, acted as poetry and arts judge in many contests, and has been the keynote speaker at art and musical festivals around the world. In 2019, he was appointed State of Kentucky Beat Poet Laureate by the National Beat Poetry Foundation (serving from 2019-2021), and he was named as the first US citizen and fourth world-wide writer-in-residence, UNESCO Tartu City of Literature international residency program, Estonia.

"Ron Whitehead is a real visionary. Ron Whitehead, out there in Kentucky, is sowing the dragon's teeth of a new heroics. Ron Whitehead is Bodhisattva in Kentucky."
-   Lawrence Ferlinghetti

"Ron Whitehead is a prophet. He is one of the world's greatest poet prophets. What an inspiring honor to hear him read here at Granada Nicaragua's International Poetry Festival!"
-   Yevgeny Yevtushenko

"Ron Whitehead is already acknowledged by many of his Elders to be a Major Literary Figure and the epitome of the work ethic! Ron and I have collaborated, recorded and performed at major festivals and universities all over the USA and Europe. Ron Whitehead is an extraordinary
motivator who inspires young people to pursue the highest standards, to work tirelessly and to celebrate the intellect by constant study of Classic Literature while remaining Creative. Ron Whitehead is one of the great lyric poets of our time. His precious Kentucky roots fill our hearts. The first time I heard Ron Whitehead read I felt what I imagine those who heard Abraham Lincoln deliver The Gettysburg Address felt. I continue to learn from him."
-   David Amram

"Ron Whitehead is one of the most exciting poets in America. Poet and literary activist, he is one of the great poets of his generation."
-   Douglas Brinkley

"I had heard people talk about Ron Whitehead for years so when I heard him read at The Ocean on the last night of the London International Poetry and Song Festival I understood why. His poems, and his reading of them, are pure genius."
-   Carolyn Cassady

"Ron Whitehead is energetic Bodhisattvic poetic spirit! Happy to see and read so much poetic energy!"
-   Allen Ginsberg

"Ron Whitehead reminds me of Corso...early Yeats in the Celtic Twilight...Ferlinghetti...Ginsberg...spontaneous transcription emerging in a tumultuous rush...infused with Whitehead's belief in the magical transformations implicit in poetry, with the music of the poem serving as chant, incantation, ultimately pagan prayer."
-   John Tytell

"I have long admired Ron Whitehead. He is crazy as nine loons, and his poetry is a dazzling mix of folk wisdom and pure mathematics."
-   Hunter S. Thompson

"Of all America's living poets - and I mean all of them, even the academic lauded ones - Ron Whitehead has the STRONGEST most PERSISTENT most POWERFUL VOICE of them all. You can hear his voice in every line, every word. It is the voice of Blake and the voice of Yeats; it is the voice of Kerouac and the voice of Ginsberg. It is the rolling thunder of Bob Dylan. It is the voice of the poet." - Dr. John Rocco

underground **books**

The View From Lawrence Ferlinghetti's Bathroom Window_

Ron **Whitehead**

printed in NYC 2019

ISBN: 978-1-7322097-1-8